Reality Check: There's a Reason Why You're Single

Reality Check: There's a Reason Why You're Single

S. Marie Brown

iUniverse, Inc.
New York Lincoln Shanghai

Reality Check: There's a Reason Why You're Single

Copyright © 2008 by S. Marie Brown

iUniverse books may be ordered through booksellers or by contacting:

iUniverse
2021 Pine Lake Road, Suite 100
Lincoln, NE 68512
www.iuniverse.com
1-800-Authors (1-800-288-4677)

Because of the dynamic nature of the Internet, any Web addresses or links contained in this book may have changed since publication and may no longer be valid.

The views expressed in this work are solely those of the author and do not necessarily reflect the views of the publisher, and the publisher hereby disclaims any responsibility for them.

ISBN: 978-0-595-48480-5 (pbk)
ISBN: 978-0-595-60572-9 (ebk)

Printed in the United States of America

I dedicate this book to my strong, hardworking, and beautiful mother.

Contents

Acknowledgments

God—"I can do ALL things through Christ who strengthens me." Phillipians 3:14 "Consider it pure joy when you face trials of many kinds for the testing of your faith builds patience." James 1:2,3. Lord, if it weren't for you speaking through me I would not be able speak to others. Thank you for giving me the courage, wisdom, and heart to write these words. You are my Lord, my Creator, my deliverer, and it is in you I trust!

Vivian Brown—You are the GREATEST mother. You are the epitome of the most loving and gracious mother. As a single mother, you show the world what it means to believe and trust that we can do ALL things with God on our side. Mom, I celebrate this first with you! I love you with all my heart.

Grandparents—Granny you are so strong and I'm so thankful for how much God has healed you. Grandaddy, you stay strong, and thank you for being a good husband. I love you two and thank you for always spoiling me.

Family—My brother, Dedre (and family), and my extended brother Jason—thanks for always being my big brothers. Uncle Terry, Auntie Angela, Cousin Julius,—Thank you for always being there for me and supporting me. Julius you're destined to be a star. Uncle Darral, Aunt Alisa, Cousin Adriel, Auntie Evelyn, Uncle Andre, Uncle Roby and family—I miss all of you and I love you dearly.

Eric White—You helped me believe in love again. Before you, I didn't know what love was, but now I know. I never learned how a real man should love until you came into my life. You love me with my "flaws and all." Wow, what a feeling! I love you, my new extended mom and dad, and my new extended family.

Erica "E-pheezie"—You know almost everything about me and have never judged me. Thank you for always being there through the good and bad times in my relationships, and for just being a great friend. You always understand me and I can always count on you for anything. I love you, girl.

Erin "Pooh" and Micah—Micah you're too young to understand now, but hopefully one day you will know Auntie S. Marie loves you. Pooh, thank you for always keeping it real—no matter what. You've been a great friend. I love you!

Robin and Brittany—Thank you for listening to me talk about my book forever. You two encouraged me and witnessed this process almost every step of the way. Thank you for the support and for your encouraging words during this entire experience. I love you two.

Shaylla, Roxy, Joseph, and Marcus (and the Mrs.)—It's good to have people from home that I know will always keep me grounded, and even keep me laughing. Though you're near and far, I can always count on your support. Thank you.

Other Friends—There's quite a few to name, but considering the fact my mind is growing seasoned, it would benefit me greatly to avoid listing everyone to ensure no one important to me is omitted. Nevertheless, all of you have, in some way, influenced me and have encouraged me throughout this entire process, and even throughout my life. Whether I grew up with you, went to church or school with you, worked with you, met you through BDC, taught with you (TFA), or met you through another friend, know that you are special to me.

Dazzling Divas of DST—I appreciate especially Xi Chapter. I also appreciate surrounding KY chapters, and all of the chapters of Delta Sigma Theta Sorority, Inc.

Church Families—Thank you to the church pastors and church families of: Shiloh (Lexington), Bracktown (Lexington), Consolidated (Lexington), Bates Memorial (Louisville), and Elizabeth—EBC (Atlanta). All of these Pastors and church families have contributed a great deal to my Christian walk through different stages of my life, which ultimately inspired my writing today.

Alison Knowlton—She is the greatest graphic designer! Alison you are talented and definitely a great person inside and out. Thank you for contributing to this project.

Ms. Jackson—Thank you for encouraging me, and for contributing your editorial skills.

Tajuana "TJ" Butler—You have truly been a role model for me. Thank you for praying with me and encouraging me through this entire process. You have so much wisdom and I sincerely appreciate all of your help and guidance.

Edwardo Jackson—Thank you for providing helpful insight throughout this process.

To my readers—Thank you to my readers and especially those who supported me prior to the release of my book. You left comments on my websites, read my blogs, and gave words of encouragement. You will definitely see me in a city near you and I look forward to having meaningful discussions and open forums.

Introduction—
Proceed with an Open Heart ...

As I talked to a number of single women, I would always hear the question, "Why I am still single?" I would even ask myself the same question. I thought, as I grew older the dating would improve, but for a period in my life it seemed like my dating life was slow and stagnant. As I experienced the ups and downs of dating, I realized I had a lot in common with so many other women. I would hear women talking all of the time about their relationships and how they couldn't find a good man. I used to go around saying, "All men are dogs! There are no good men left." Of course I wasn't alone because there were plenty of other women who agreed with me. Usually the conversations I had or heard revolved around male bashing, but those discussions would later change.

Through personal experiences and my observations of others, something caught my attention. No matter what the situation and no matter what occurred in the unhealthy relationships, there was always one common denominator. I noticed there was in fact a reason why I and many other women were still single. It was like reality had set in because I really had to keep it real with myself about some issues. Nevertheless, *Reality Check: There's a Reason Why You're Single* was born and now I want to share it with you.

When I began writing, I had so many different types of people in my mind. I thought of the single women who were tired of being single. I thought of single women who were still dealing with the hurts and pains caused by the divorce and the breakups. I thought of the single women who were giving up hope on finding Mr. Right. I thought about the single mothers still hoping to find a loving and family man. I thought about the married women who could easily reflect on how challenging their single life used to be before entering the wonderful union of marriage. Not only did I think about single women, but I also thought about the single men who are in fact trying to do right and still looking for Mrs. Right. I thought about all of these people and wanted to find a way to ensure everyone—whether single or married—could relate to the topic of "being single."

Please understand you must approach the book with a sincere heart and a willingness to keep it real about every situation that has occurred in your life. I definitely share personal stories and experiences that some would be embarrassed to share. However, when it comes to helping others through a storm, what better way to help them than to share how you overcame the storm. I want us, as women, to be open and honest with ourselves instead of putting on a façade. I wanted other women to know that I've been through the same obstacles and I've definitely had my share of hurts and pains. Moreover, it was important for me to also share that we don't have to wallow in our past pains forever. Bitterness, anger, and negative attitudes towards dating doesn't have to follow us throughout the rest of our lives—no matter how many dead relationships we've experienced. Obviously, I experienced different situations in my life so I could be a testimony as to what God can bring us through, and so I could help others see the power living within them through God.

Do not be confused. This is **not** a blame game for men or women; rather it is a Reality Check that is long overdue. I re-emphasize that you must approach this book with a sincere heart and a willingness to be open with yourself. You will have to reflect on the good and the bad, and remove all of the negative feelings that are clogging up your heart. There will be situations discussed and you'll say to yourself, "Wow. I see myself in that situation. She is talking about me because I've been through the same thing." Men, you will also see yourself in some of the situations, which may cause you to take a deeper look within yourself to determine the type of man you really are. Overall, each person will relate to it in some way. Make sure you complete the realistic thinking activities following each reality checkpoint in order to reflect on what you've read.

Be prepared to laugh, cry, reflect, keep it real, and most importantly be empowered. You are about to experience Reality Check: There's a Reason Why You're Single, and you might be surprised to know why.

Enjoy,
S. Marie

Reality Checkpoints

1—You choose to do your own thing instead of God's thing, and allow your man to be everything.

2—You equate love with sex, but what's love got to do with lust?

3—Previous "cats" you've dated before make you think of your present one as a dog.

4—You think of him as a piece of clay you will be able to mold into what you want him to be.

5—Trying to keep up with the Joneses'—also known as your girlfriends.

6—Expectations and standards sound more like ultimatums.

7—"I think, therefore I am—LONELY."

8—Looking for money, mansions, and mo' money instead of man.

9—Trying to turn boys into men.

10—Over 30 and worried.

11—Reality Check 101

Reality Checkpoint #1—*You choose to do your own thing instead of God's thing, and allow your man to be everything.*

Imagine it's the beginning of the ending of a relationship. It seems like your time, energy, and sacrifices were all wasted away. You are sitting, pondering, and trying to figure out what happened. In the beginning everything seemed so right, but it ended so wrong. In the beginning you were happy and content with everything, and now you sit wondering why your heart hurts so much. You don't really feel like you did anything to mess up the relationship. In fact, you feel you prayed and did what you were supposed to do. You even prayed, "Lord let thy will be done. If it's in your will let it be." For some reason, however, it just didn't work out.

This common prayer we have prayed time and time again, but do we really mean it? What are we really asking for? Could we really and truly recognize God's will even if he put it right in front of us? Sometimes it may be right in our face, but we ignore or hide from it. If God's will is to be done, you have to be sure you refrain from focusing all of your attention on finding your dream man, your dream job, your dream house, dream vacation, or even your dream pet, and instead focus on His will.

When we pray this simple prayer, "Lord let thy will be done," we are submitting fully to Christ and what He has in store for us. We are committing ourselves to follow His path for our lives. The prayer is easy to say, but difficult to put into action when the time comes. When we first meet our guy, in the beginning this may be the prayer we send up to God because we are so excited about finding a new man. We're like, "Lord, thank you so much for finally sending him. This must be it." Maybe only a month or even days have passed and we automatically assume he is the one. However, do we still believe in this prayer throughout the relationship, and even after the relationship has ended? For instance, we meet a new man and immediately we say, "Lord let thy will be done," but then we place the Lord on the back burner to ensure every precious moment of our time is devoted mainly to the new "love of our lives." We wake up on Sunday morning and choose to lay with his arms around us instead of choosing to spend time with the Lord for morning worship service. Wednesday arrives and we decide bible study is no competition for a nice romantic dinner with our "boo." Ministry time is interrupted because of the excessive time we spend with our significant other. Prayer and meditation have been replaced with kisses and QT (quality time). Earlier we prayed the simple prayer "Lord let thy will be done," but now we find ourselves asking if God is truly in this relationship and is

His will truly being completed? We run to Him for comfort and confirmation when we decide it is convenient for us to confer with God.

Quality Time with the One who Matters Most

True worship occurs through personal relationship with God. The more time you spend with your significant other, the more you get to know him. Of course the same is true with the Lord. To know Him is to love him and vice versa. Something must be sacrificed in order to make room for a new priority. I can remember spending hours upon hours and sometimes days upon days with men from my past relationships. All I wanted to do was be with them and be by their side for more reasons than one. Sometimes the time was spent doing idle things, or even doing things that would prevent me from growing closer to God. I know how it feels to think you're so in love and to only want to spend time with him, and truly enough that's how in love we should be with God. We should yearn and desire to know the one who truly controls our destiny. Many times we spend so much time with our significant other that we miss out on other opportunities. Instead of studying longer in order to the pass your class with an A, you decide to stay cuddled up in the bed all day. Instead of being productive and spending more time finding a different career choice, we decide to follow his dreams instead of our own. Instead of making time for your friends and family we find ways to cater more to his needs than what our family may even need. We sacrifice time and energy that could be so useful in different aspects of our lives. Now don't misunderstand me because quality time is crucial for any type of relationship. However, you cannot dedicate 24/7 to someone you merely consider your boyfriend, and expect the rest of your areas of your life to be complete and whole. Your relationship may be full and alive, while everything else around you appears to be dead.

A married couple is considered one and everything should be 50:50, and in dating the compromise should be the same. Nonetheless, we as women sometimes think we need to do all the work and dedicate ALL of our time to someone who we truly know is/may not be the one. We basically decide to devote ourselves to that person and sometimes only to make sure no one else is spending quality time with them. Then, the relationship ends all together. We lose what we once thought of as "our everything" only to forget that everything comes solely from God. Don't allow yourself to spend more time with him and less time with the

Heavenly Father because the same God we forget about during the relationship will be the same God we'll need when it's all said and done and the relationship is brought to a close. If God is going to bless you, you should want to do what you can to make Him want to bless you. Do not simply take advantage of his grace and mercy. We don't deserve anything He does, but the least we could do is give of our time, our love, and simply our best!

If you were in a relationship that was 80:20 with you doing all the work, you probably started to feel like you were the only one in the relationship. Nevertheless, you might have even given up trying to please that man because you realized you were doing all of the work. No one likes to feel as if they're being taken advantage of, or as if the love is not being reciprocated. So, if your relationship with God is 80:20, how do you think He feels? How do you think the One who gave His only son for someone who gives nothing? Thank God for His mercy because in spite of our lack of personal devotion time we spend with Him, He still manages to bless us and keep us. Our actions easily reveal our deepest passions and those things we really want to do. If you enjoy pursuing men no matter when and where, then your mind will be consumed with those things. However, John tells us that if we pursue the Kingdom of God *first* then all other things will be added unto us. If your heart and mind is focused on serving others and being a diligent worker to help the Kingdom of God, then God will bless you for being faithful and for being a helpful steward to benefit His kingdom. God has to know we are serious about doing His will. He must know that when he does bless us with the man, the job, the money, then we will not forget Him and become proud and boastful.

I remember when I dated a guy in college and we were pursuing an independent selling business; rather he was pursuing the business and I in turn decided I wanted to pursue the business also. I was so into him and what he was into that I decided to do it also, but I completely forgot all of my priorities. Going to church, worship services, and even my college classes were a regular part of my routine, but quickly I began making excuses. I used the business as my scapegoat to justify my reasoning for not going to church. "I have to make money, of course, because God wants me to be prosperous and feed my children's children". Yes, God wants me to live an abundant and prosperous life, but not at the expense of living without Him. We must understand that to live prosperous does not automatically mean to have riches and money.

During this time, my grades also began to fail as I was spending less time studying and going to classes. Why? I was too busy attending business trips and trying to earn money in order to provide for myself, and the buy the extra outfits, the shoes—nothing with any true value. All of my life I dreamt of not only attending college but graduating from college because I was going to be one of the few in my family to accomplish this goal. Soon I began to notice my dream drifting into the field of hopeless dreams—the place where dreams lie dead and dormant because people did not have the courage to conquer them. I remember wondering if I was living my dream or simply going along with everything in order to please him. It was easy for me to say yes I support you, but when it came time to support my dreams and what I wanted to do, the support didn't return as easily. He thought I was wasting my time by trying to graduate from college. He concluded that I was only setting myself up to become the worker of someone else; so he thought it was better for me to participate in the business more so I would have a solid future. I believe and support entrepreneurship, but the business for me was not going as well as planned. The only problem was the business, for me, was not going as well as planned. After three months passed, I was not as successful as I had been in the beginning. Money and clients were not coming in as easily and I was putting in more money than I was receiving. I was blinded by the potential fame and fortune, which made it easy to get distracted. All I wanted to do was follow my partner's plans, and make him happy by doing what he wanted to do. Yes, he encouraged me to stick with it, but it was my decision to continue despite the constant front I put on for my family, friends, and clients.

Eventually I realized my purpose for being in college and decided to focus my attention on what God truly intended for me. God had not brought me through college this far just to have me quit and give up. Even then it was difficult to take myself away from the business and it was even more difficult to take myself away from the relationship; but I had to do it. I had to do it for me, my family, my friends, my children, and even for you! No, I haven't met you personally but I had to do it for you so that through my past experiences and lessons learned you will find strength even now to be able to tell him your dreams and what exactly it is God wants to do in your life. You don't have to sit in the dark and ignore your dreams because your man wants you to. You can make enough time to spend with your Father and your man.

Through prayer and fasting I was able to hear from God and be refreshed in knowing what His plan was for me. Through His mercy and grace I graduated from college and fulfilled the vision I once dreamed years before in spite of almost giving up on what I knew was for me. We will always have obstacles and mishaps along our journey, but we have to remember to go to God and allow him to get us back on track.

When it's all said and done

It's not only when we are in the relationship when our attention is focused solely on the man. Even months after the relationship has ended, we find ourselves still dedicated to him and placing all of our focus and attention on him. Here are some thoughts that easily occupy our minds:

"I wonder what he's doing."

"She's not good enough for him. She's not like me at all."

"I'm going to make him pay for what he did to me."

"I can't believe he would do this to me after all we've been through."

"I wonder if I should call him."

"I don't care. He knows he loves me and we'll be back together."

"He's just young. He'll grow up and learn and he'll be begging for me to get back with him." We debate back and forth whether to call, or we even make the declaration that when he calls we will not answer the phone—no matter what. We even go as far as to delete the number from the phone. Then, as soon as his number appears on our phone—yes we deleted the number but can still recognize it miles away because we called it only 50 million times—we are quick to answer the phone hoping for some type of chance or reunion despite the declaration we made. We go out with our friends or even to church and pray that we see him just to get a glimpse of him or vice versa hoping that he will see our true beauty and want to be back with us. The list goes on and on and on.

Our mindset affects our actions, feelings, and how we speak because ultimately we can't hide the way we really feel. Of course you have to take time and deal with any hurt and pain you may be dealing with, but when we put all of our energy into him, even after it's all said and done, we find ourselves feeling sad, guilty, hurt, and even depressed. We lay in our beds crying our eyes out because we feel so hurt. We make excuses and even blame ourselves for everything that happened. We become depressed and forget that life does go on with or without him. We show signs of weakness instead of being the strong women that God created us to be. This is not to say that sometimes people do work things out, but I'm talking to that girl, lady, or woman who knows it is time for her to leave him alone but is seeking to find the strength to just do it. Sweetheart, I've been there and I know the strength that lies within you. Bring it to life and stand on your declaration that you will not dedicate your whole being to him, but will dedicate your whole being to the real HIM—God. He will give you the strength you need to overcome the weakness that prevents you from letting go. The longer you wait, the more you're preventing yourself from going to the next level in your life.

There are times when we play the guilt trip and throw self-pity parties in order to try and make sense of what happened. Nevertheless, this is usually the time when God wants us to reach out to Him for His love, protection, and security. We should know that God loves us more than we love ourselves. Besides, do you really think most men are sitting around gloomy and sad months and months after the break-up? Yes, they may feel pain and heartache, but their lives do not stop and yours does not have to either. Women are naturally more emotional, but we do not have to let our emotions take complete control over our lives. If your focus remains on those things in the past, then how can God bless you into your future destiny? How can His will be fulfilled when you're not willing to move forward (We will deal with this issue more in the chapter that relates to previous cats we have dated before)?

There was a time when I couldn't let go of someone for an entire year. Yes, I said it—an entire year. For an entire year I played mind games with myself and continued having this false hope of him wanting me back. Unfortunately, part of the problem was my willingness to allow him to play games with me. I allowed him to control my life instead of submitting to God and his plans for my life. He would tell me all the things I wanted to hear. For example, he would say things like:

"Even though I'm with her, I don't care about her like I care about you. I THINK we could be back together in the future. Yes, I still love you. I'll never stop loving you. I just need time to figure some things out." All of these things and more were said, and I would use them to support the notion that we would eventually be back together. He had moved on with another woman and everything, and I still had this false hope of thinking that I was the one that was supposed to be in his life. I was practically willing to wait for him for the rest of my life at that time because at the time I thought he was supposed to be in my life. God was trying to show me that he was not meant for me, but I ignored anyone who tried to convince me otherwise. I was so convinced that I was the best girlfriend he ever had, and there was no way he would want to be with someone other than me.

Throughout the year I was caught up with reading books that told the story of lovers brought back together through fate or what I thought was God's will. Ironically, I was only interested in these books because he was also reading the same books. I secretly thought he was trying to hint to me how much he cared about me by comparing himself to different characters in the book. I used to think the same things that were taking place in the stories would happen in my real life story. I would try to date other men, but in the back of my mind I thought I was just passing away time until he came back into my life. Deep down inside I was just trying to cover up my true feelings and act as if I was content with the situation. You know how it is sometimes. You have to put on a façade for your friends—especially your girlfriends, but even my closest friends could see through it all. I

I just knew he would see the light and would ask for a reunion despite the fact that I knew we truly were not meant to be with each other. It was not completely his fault and it never is because I was not complete in every aspect of my life also. Furthermore, in the midst of making someone else "our everything," God will sometimes find a way to lead us back to Him. I would say to myself, "I know he wants me because his mother loves me. We've been involved for too long. He just needs time to figure out what he wants. He just needs some time away from me so he can get his 'player' habits out of his system, which will keep him from later cheating on me." However, I was the one cheating myself. I was cheating myself out of happiness and the true joy that could only be provided from above. On the outside I was hiding it but hurting deep within. I couldn't tell my girlfriends that I was still thinking about him, or that I wanted him in my life. They would think I was wasting time on him, and during that time I didn't want to hear the truth. I ignored the truth in order to support my strong belief that we would eventually get back together. It seems so far fetched that someone could hold onto someone for so long, but since we're keeping it real that's the reality of so many women.

Lord, is this you?

Sometimes men say they need time, but we're not willing to give that time to them because we think this is it, and we are hesitant to give up on what we think could be our last chance at love. God always has a plan for everything so if it is meant to be then it truly will be. The funny part is that I actually did know this but I didn't want to face reality. I wanted to force something to happen instead of waiting for God's plan to be revealed. I wish I would have known how to apply this to my situation during the time I was actually going through it, but that's why I'm writing to you today.

Ladies, I want to tell you that you don't have to sit around wondering if he's coming back, thinking about what he's doing, worrying about his new girlfriend, contemplating if he's your husband or not, wondering if he misses you, concerned with how his life is going, or debating if he is as unhappy as you are. If it is meant to be it will be. It is not worth putting your life on hold just to indulge your mind, body, and soul into a relationship that eventually you will realize was never a part of God's plan to begin with.

There were times I would even ask, "Is this you, Lord? Is this a part of your plan for me? Give me a sign, Lord, so I'll know whether it's from you." Yes, I prayed this prayer but as soon as the sign, or even signs, would come I would ignore them. I would act as if they were merely acts of coincidences. Some would even tell me straight to my face that they didn't want to be with me and I would still try to work things out. I would see through their lies and deceit or the Lord would just speak to me directly and tell me that this was not a part of his plan. Yet and still I ignored the signs and attempted to follow my own agenda. I wanted to be with a man and escape the single life no matter what I had to do. My agenda, however, would later backfire and accomplish nothing in the end. Now, I laugh at that situation only because I cannot believe the numerous amounts of excuses I would make for myself. I've always known that excuses were useless, but at that time I was willing to argue anything to support my theory. I would make excuses such as the Lord doesn't want me to be single and sometimes you have to have patience in order to get what you want. Well, I was being patient but not for what God wanted me to have. I felt it was worth the risk to be patient for my ex, but clearly when it's time for me to be patient with God for something it was as if I doubted His power and ability to stand on His word. I was not patient enough to sit still and let God do his work. Instead I tried to rush the process and force what I thought was His plan into existence. It was obvious that it was not in God's plans for me to be with him, but sometimes we ignore God speaking just to make sure our plans are carried out.

Our heart's desires

We continue to contradict our prayers with our actions because we truly and honestly don't want to do God's will; rather, we feel as if we would be satisfied with fulfilling the will we think is best for us at that time. You have to admit that at the end of the day, we do what we truly and honestly want to do. It is a harsh reality, but so important to understand. If your friends ask you to go to the movies, to the mall, or even to a game usually your response will be yes because you find those things interesting to do or because you enjoy shopping. However, if your friends were to ask you to do something you honestly did not want to do with no questions asked, most likely you would refuse. Why? You did not want to participate and you were not interested. You refused to go to the concert or the show because you truly did not want to go.

Our heart's desires are easily visible through our actions and words. How we spend our time, our money, and our energy is direct reflection of our hearts' desires. If you desire a man, you will pursue after a man. If you desire money, you will constantly pursue after things that will bring about money. If you pursue a job, a house, or your dream car you will do just that—pursue it. If, however, you desire to do God's will instead of your own, then your actions and attitude will easily reflect that. We have to quit thinking our way is the best way all of the time and instead be more submissive to His will. It's so unfortunate to follow merely our selfish desires because eventually we see how our decisions to merely do what *we want* impact the rest of our lives. Moreover, the time we spend doing what we want right now will forever be irreplaceable.

Sick and Tired of Being Sick and Tired—Release!

Although time was lost and I spent much of it doing what I wanted, it wasn't too late for me to get things back in order and it is not too late for you also. Earlier I mentioned how I spent a year with this false hope of getting back with him. After the year finally passed I realized our relationship was actually over. I had a reality check, ladies. What exactly happened that brought me to this point? Well, there comes a time when you are sick of being sick and that is basically what happened. I was fed up with being fed up. I was tired of always calling and checking up on him. I was tired of waiting for him to come around. I was tired of hearing the excuses as to why two people who were supposedly in love could not be together. I was tired of feeling like I was doing all of the work while he was moving on with his life. I was all the more tired of my mind being occupied with nothing but thoughts of him. It was time for a "renewing of my mind" and a transformation. I wanted to experience the abundance of true joy and focus on those things that would bring life, not sadness and depression.

For a long time I blamed everyone else for what was going on during that year. The male bashing started and I started talking bad about every man. It wasn't until later in my life that I acknowledged it was actually my fault for remaining in bondage because I was allowing the chains from the relationship to keep me there. No, it was not the devil as we try to blame for all of the bad in our lives, and I know God was bringing me through it, but it was not God who caused the hurt and pain I endured during this time. I couldn't just blame my ex for the pain I endured also because it was my decision to put all of my energy and effort into this situation. I took ownership of my life and soon realized that I was the one who decided to remain in bondage for as long as I did. I was the one who decided to put all of my effort into someone who did not even make the ultimate sacrifice by dying for my sins. I refer to these types of situations as bondage because anything in our lives that keeps us from moving forward can easily be thought of as chains holding us down. Chains limit our abilities and where we can go. They limit the potential blessings that God has in store for us because our spiritual minds and bodies are not prepared for the next level of blessings. Moreover, I was limited as far as where I could go because I allowed myself to stay in that same spot for a year! I couldn't even try to be with someone else or hear God speaking to me because I was so pre-consumed with trying to work out the past dealings of my life. My everything revolved around him as I neglected the true Him—God. How can you move forward while looking back? You've probably seen on television or even in real life when a mouse gets caught in a mousetrap and struggles to get out, and sometimes it dies right there in that same location. The mouse ends up dying because he lacks the nutrients and daily necessities to sustain his health. We could potentially end up just like that little mouse if we continue to remain in our current state because we will deprive ourselves of our daily needs such as grace, joy, peace, blessed assurance, healing, and love. Instead, we'll end up feeding ourselves depression, sadness, and things that will deprive us of a healthy and happy life. We can't keep asking God to move in our lives and bless us if we have the desire to remain in the same state. Those who want to move on will do so and those who do not will not.

We have heard the cliché time and time again but it means so much more, "Let go and let God." You have to let go of whatever you are trying to hold onto and allow God to manifest His self into your mind, body, and spirit. You may be in a situation right now trying to get over your past lover. Release that chain! Your dad may have never told you he loved you so you are looking for love in all the wrong places. Release that chain! You may be struggling with sexual immorality when you know you want to live a more pure life. Release that chain! You may feel like you will never find a man because you are still holding onto the hurt and pain your ex lovers caused you. Release that chain! Whatever chains you are holding onto right now—ex-lover, fatherless home, sexual immorality, sexual molestation, divorce, obesity, low self-esteem, drugs, alcohol, failure, and any others—release those chains and move into your destiny that God is calling you into.

Mean what you say, and do what you say.

"Let thy will be done" is a simple prayer we can pray with our mouths, yet requires a dramatic change in our hearts, minds, and behavior. Our desires should coincide with our prayers, actions, and most importantly God's will. We can't pray this prayer and then question God's authority or his plans. It is not enough to pray this prayer, yet decide to ignore him when he speaks to us. If we spend more time with God, then we will be able to discern between God speaking and the world speaking. In order for His will to be done, we must courageously accept whatever God has for us. It can be difficult at times but think about all of the times we've accepted the plans of others and have even lowered our standards just to please them. With God we are not lowering our standards; rather we are going to the next level in our lives through His power and guidance. He knows what's best for us better than we know ourselves. If it's love, joy, and even healing from past relationships that you need, He is the one that can supply it. Going from man to man will not restore the broken pieces of your heart.

If you want to walk into your future, then you cannot make your man everything, and accept God as nothing. It has been said for some time, "If you going to talk the talk, then walk the walk." Moreover, I say if you are going to pray the prayer, then rely on God to take you there. Follow God and truly make your life about doing his will, and not your will. Matthew reminds us to "Seek ye first the Kingdom of God and all other things will be added unto you." If you seek God's Kingdom and serve Him, then your steps will truly be ordered by him, and all other things will be provided according to His will—your house, your finances, your success, your family, and yes, even your husband.

Reality Speaks: Only the Real ONE can do for you,
what NO ONE else can do for you.

<u>Realistic Thinking</u>

How many hours in a day, or days in a week, do you spend with your partner?

_____

_____

_____

_____

Fill in this empty pie chart to show the percentage of time you allo-cate to different activities/areas of your life during a typical day/week (which ever one is easier).

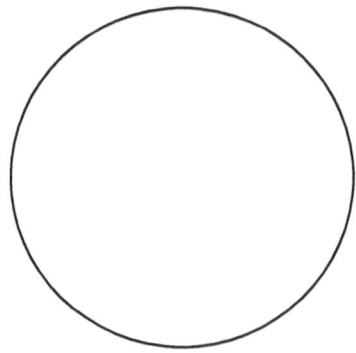

Which areas of my life—school, career, family, spirituality, etc.—have I neglected because of the time I've spent with my partner?

_____

_____

_____

_____

_____

_____

_____

Today, I commit to spend at least (write down the number of minutes, hours, days you plan to allocate your time for different activities):

_____

_____

_____

_____

<u>Reality Checkpoint #2</u>—*You equate love with sex, but what's love got to do with lust?*

"Oooh … he is so fine over there. Look at him. I would so give it up to him. I wonder if he's good in the bed. She can't do it like I can. He needs a real woman to show it how it is done."

These statements, although sexually explicit, have been made by plenty of women at a lounge, while dancing at the club, or at any other type of event. Imagine with me for a moment. You have set your eyes on him and have decided he will be the next one you give it up to. You have decided that he is going to be your "baby daddy." When we refer to "give it up," it is another way of saying I would have sex with that man. We see something in his eyes, mouth, legs, arms, or even abs that starts the process of sexual temptation. Immediately our minds begin to wonder impure sexual thoughts and eventually lead to a sexual encounter.

As you think you are only referring to giving up the goods, you are actually confirming the reality of the situation once the sexual encounter takes place. Literally you are giving it up, but you are giving up more than just "the goods". You are giving up your dignity, your security, your love, your secret wonder, your spirit, your time, and simply put, you. You are giving up your temple (your body), which really belongs to God and giving it to someone who could care less about your temple. Furthermore, you are giving a part of you that will never be returned back to you. It is almost like a deal without a real deal— you give it up and receive nothing in return. Yes, it is a new millennium and sex has become one of the main priorities for people in their lives and their relationships, but the Bible teaches us that we are not to conform to this world, especially when we are conforming to something that will not bring us life. The unfortunate realization of it all is the fact that we will or have given up something that can NEVER be replaced. Although it cannot be replaced, we can find a way to change the outcome of future situations. Many of us have ruined countless numbers of relationships because we concluded that more sex meant more love. FYI, x doesn't equal y, and casual sex doesn't equal love. We decided that sex would be the determining factor of how well or poor our relationship would be even though we were not prepared for the consequences that would come later. We have even tricked ourselves into thinking that we can have sex with a man and not have feelings for him. We figure we will be strong so we can get the money, the clothes, the love, or merely attention. It may start off that way; but somehow in the end we end up falling even harder for him when we engage in sexual relations.

What do you really love?

So how do we get ourselves into the predicament of sexual temptation? A typical situation usually occurs when two people meet and of course an immediate attraction is made. They may talk for a few hours on the phone and engage in small talk, real talk, or even sex talk. No matter what type of talk usually the discussion of sex arises. He might spark a flame by repeatedly complementing us, talking about his love for Christ and his family, mention how he is looking for a good woman, and how he is tired of being hurt. Instantly he appeals to our desires because he seems like a "good man" who causes us to feel even more attracted to him. We feel like some type of connection has been made and he seems like the perfect guy because he is saying all the right things. Remember, however, sometimes people will say what they want to get what they want. Next thing you know you are on the first date or even at his apartment on the first night and the exchange is made—exchange of sexual relaxation and pleasure. The process of getting to know each other is placed on the backburner while personal satisfaction and gratitude takes first priority. At that time it seems like a plan that could work, but in the end it could have negative repercussions.

One of the common mistakes we as women make is equating love with sex. We consider the exchange as his way of exchanging his heart with ours. We think we have definitely met our match because the sex was so passionate and it actually felt good. Well, reality check; God intended for sex to be a pleasant experience between a husband and a wife. So, the feelings we have when we engage in the sexual experience are natural, yet still intended for the right time in our lives. Many relationships have been destroyed because of the inclusion of sex. We failed to understand how our feelings were confused because we included sex as a part of the relationship. We used our feelings to guide our actions and behavior. Ladies, we have to know that we are emotional creatures by nature and it is in us to feel overly compassionate and loving towards other people. Nevertheless, we have to be careful and guard our hearts and minds to prevent trickery and charm from deceiving us into thinking we are in love. So, he is fine and looks great in a suit or even dressed down, but what is he really about? How can you be in love with someone you don't even know, and how can he truly know who you are? All you know about him at this point is whether or not he can give you great pleasure in the bedroom. To love someone is to know someone, and we have to do a better job of getting to know our mates without using sex as the determining factor.

Another common mistake occurs when we consider sex as something we need in order to release and feel less tense, but the consequences are rarely considered during the moment of passion. We ignore the fact that one passionate moment could affect more than one moment of our lives, and even the rest of our lives. Once we engage in sexual intercourse, no longer are we intimate with the person we are trying to know, but we are intimate with the pleasure for which he provides to us. We are in love with the act of being in love. When two people are in love and married, making love is something they share between each other as a symbol of their love for each other. We, on the other hand, perform sexual acts with people we barely know and talk about marriage later. Then, when the time comes to really get to know each other, a struggle between lust and love occurs. I have talked with many women and men who continuously stay with their partner in spite of their horrible personalities or character. When asked why they chose to stay, they openly admitted they stayed because the sex was good and it was convenient. They were considered convenient because they were always there when they needed it or they were always there when they wanted some "good loving". Wow! We have come to a moment in time where we are willing to stay with someone who we know were not created to be our helpmate just to satisfy the yearning and desire for the STD, AIDS, HIV, cervical cancer provider—sex? Are we willing to continuously risk what God has for us just for a moment of satisfaction? If so, it shows how much less, if at all, we value ourselves.

As I reflected over the years, I studied the mistakes in past relationships and the reasons why most of those relationships failed. I soon realized that sex played a huge role in so many different areas of my relationships in a negative way. I considered those times when I was so paranoid that my boyfriend was cheating on me; and, when I say paranoid I mean paranoid. I would constantly wonder what he was doing or I would find myself checking his phone for missed calls or text messages from other females. Then, to further support my paranoia I would say that men could not be trusted and I need to do this to make sure he is not cheating. Now, unfortunately there were times when it was true and he was in fact cheating, but I would not always find the truth in his phone. Furthermore, I just knew I did not want him with another woman because I wanted to be the only woman satisfying him. Because I had engaged in sexual relations, I was connected to him, and could not fathom the idea of him being with another female in the same way. As sad as it may seem, I actually wanted to be the one he talked to his boys about, but for the wrong reasons. I figured he would feel proud to have someone like me. Some of you may be thinking now, "Wow! It was that bad?" Reality check: There are many other women who feel the same way I felt.

I even thought because we engaged in sexual contact it was evident how much we loved each other. Let's think, however, how different these feelings would have been had the sex not been a part of the relationship. I know for a fact things would have been different because I would not have let the sex determine how strong my feelings were for him. I would have spent less time engaging in sexual activities and more time getting to know the real person on the inside. That may sound like a cliché but honestly, how are we to become one with a person without truly getting to know who they are? Just because you have sex with your boyfriend does not guarantee a deeper exchange of feelings, and a better relationship. For the most part, the only thing casual sex (not sex between a man and his wife) guarantees is a risk for something unexpected or harmful to occur. As women we have to understand we are more emotional than men and when we think we can just have sex without feelings, we are fooling ourselves. Think about how many times you submitted to a man by having sex and later realized he was not your type at all. You thought to yourself, "Why was I with him anyway? Or what was I thinking?" You were thinking "Oh my goodness I'm so in love with him," when you failed to realize that love was nowhere in the relationship. We have even questioned, after it was over, why we allowed ourselves to do it when we knew it was not the right thing to do. Unfortunately, Sex controlled your feelings and caused you to ignore the real person within.

More than love lost

Many times you have probably heard people say that when women have sex with a man too soon, the man loses respect for her, and for the most part that is true. He now looks at you as any of the other girls he dated, and you do not set yourself apart from anyone else. Nevertheless, the woman is actually losing respect for herself also because she does not think enough of herself to wait or say no. How much are you respecting yourself by choosing to "give up the goods" to this man, the next man, and the next man after him? Eventually you will forget where you left your "goods" before you move onto the next man, and when you finally meet your husband your goods could totally be corrupted.

Not only do we lose respect from others and respect for ourselves, but we also distance ourselves from God. Once the act(s) have taken place, it does something to us physically, mentally, and spiritually. First, our sinful lifestyles separate us from God. It becomes difficult to go to God and ask for what we need when we know we have not been living a righteous life. Secondly, we lose of course something we can never get back. We can always alter our lifestyles, but the pleasure of sharing something so precious with our husbands is forever taken away. Some of us even regret our mistakes and look back wondering how things would have been different. Thirdly, our sexual lifestyle sometimes alters and modifies our life plans. Diseases, illnesses, pregnancies, or other things alter what we thought was going to take place in our lives. Lastly, the sexual lifestyle for many will tarnish a reputation. In a society where men are praised for the number of women they sleep with, women are usually the first to be condemned for their promiscuity. Understand that you may gain a new man and exciting sexual relationship, but you take the risk of losing your life—spiritually, emotionally, and physically.

Sexual needs or just sexual pleasure

This sub heading helps to explain one of the reasons why we find ourselves engaging in sex when we know deep down inside that's not what we want. Sometimes we engage in sex because we think that is what we HAVE to do in order for him to like us. As powerful and strong as we appear to be on the outside, we still may be weak and silent on the inside because we don't know how to stand up and just say no.

"He is so fine. He could probably get it from anyone but he chose me. I know he will not be with me if I tell him I don't want to have sex. He will think I am weird if I don't do it. I have to have sex with him to show him I am the best he has ever had, and then I know he will want to be with me."

Some, if not all, are thoughts we have considered when fighting through the struggle of having or refraining from sex. We go back and forth in our minds and have this debate with ourselves trying to figure out what to do. We say these statements to justify why having sex with him is necessary for the development of our relationship. We actually think if we have sex then everything will be okay between the two of us. Furthermore, we remind ourselves that he is a man and we have to supply his needs, because if we don't then someone else will; but have we considered the fact that it is not our full responsibility to take care of his needs especially if he is not our husband? We are so committed to fulfilling his needs that we forget to supply our own needs for purity and righteousness. For those who are content with giving up their goods, you may think sex is not all that bad, but I am seriously talking to those women who have declared they are tired of giving up their goods and really want to try and be abstinent or maintain their virginity. Please know that sex is not necessary for the relationship—especially in the beginning. Quit thinking it is necessary in order for the relationship to be interesting and fun. Yes, it helps satisfy each other's desires, but at the end of the day you should want to satisfy God. Quit asking Him to do everything while you do nothing to please Him. If you do not want it in your relationship then you don't have to compromise your beliefs and submit to his will, but instead you can choose to submit to the will of God, the one that really matters.

Many times we ask God to bless our relationship and do whatever to help us stay together, but we refuse to honor God by obeying His commands. We pray, "Lord help us stay together. Let this one be the one, Lord, and I promise I will not mess it up." It is like your partner coming to you and asking you to pay his mortgage, buy his clothes, pay his cell phone bills, or just spend time with him. Although he asks for these things, he refuses to give you the same in return. You would be upset and would probably refuse everything because you would feel like he doesn't deserve it. Moreover, why should God bless your relationship and you do not even adhere to his word or do anything for Him? You are left wondering why the relationship has ended or why you two cannot seem to work things out. Admit that up until now it has only been about you and how you feel because even though you know you should obey God's word, you are only concerned about receiving pleasure and giving it to a man who may not even be worth it.

Another reason we engage in sexual relations is because we think of it as a way to build our low self-esteem. A lot of times we judge each other as women and immediately refer to a woman who sleeps around as a "hoe." I ask you, however, are there any differences between a woman who sleeps around once or twice a year, and a woman who sleeps around once or twice a week? Yes, one is having sex more than the other, but if you looked at their self-esteem through a microscope you would see that both women are yearning for admiration, affection, and attention. You want someone to admire your looks, someone to hold, and just someone there who will listen. These are things of course you look for in your potential mate, but you have to make sure you love yourself whether the admiration, affection, and attention from a man are there or not. Both women are looking for the assurance of a man who says, "Yes, baby, you are the best. I love you. You are beautiful:" all of which mean nothing if it is based primarily on how well you perform in the bedroom.

Our fatherless homes may have even played a role in our low self-esteem, which helps to explain why we yearn so deeply for a love we have never experienced from any type of man. Yet and still, our fathers are not all to blame, but could have contributed to our confusion of knowing the true love a real man. Some of us, including myself, lacked the guidance from a father to tell us how a man should treat a woman, and how to tell if a man truly loved us. I was on a quest to find a man who was the opposite of my father because I wanted to experience love in a real way. I would constantly worry about finding a good man because I did not want my children to grow up without a father; yet, I was looking for the men to do what only my Heavenly Father could do. I would tell my ex's that I needed reassurance and I needed to know that he thought I was beautiful and loved me, when all the while I should have been the reassurance for myself. We have to be the one to stand in front of the mirror and say we are beautiful in spite of what we look like, and not allow the numbers of times we have sex to dictate how beautiful we think we are. So your father was not in your life; but even one hundred sexual encounters will not bring you any more love than he could have even if your father had been in your life. Eventually, you will find yourself on a path of giving up the goods to everyone in hopes of finding an invisible treasure that will never be discovered.

Another reason we tend to engage in sexual relations is usually because of the simple phrase known as "everybody's doing it." We've heard this for years now, but recently this phrase has a lot more meaning because we live in a society where the majority accepts sexual immorality, whether young or old. Right now I want you to think of how many of your closest friends (your ride or die chicks, your best friends, your girlfriends, etc.) are having sex, and how many times you all have talked about how wrong it is, but how much you just cannot stop doing it because it feels so good. Peer pressure was something we used to think of as only occurring when we were younger, but it still affects us even as we grow older. You know you and the girls sit around and talk about your sexual escapades because I would do the same things, but there are those who really want to open up and tell each other that they want to try and get things in order in their lives by abstaining from sex. What prevents you from speaking up? What keeps you from keeping it real with the girls who you have been friends with for years? It is a thing we refer to as fear—fear of their response and how they will perceive you. You fear they will think you are crazy or trying to be a "holy roller," or you fear they will reject your decision and not support your thoughts and opinions.

While it is natural to feel that way, understand that any person you choose to make a part of your life, whether it's male or female, should be the kind of person who will inspire you to be better and live better. I have heard time and time again, if you hang around 9 broke people, you are bound to be the 10th broke person. Why? You are not surrounding yourself around those who strive to better themselves, or who have the strength to stand up for what they know is right. So, ultimately you become like them because you will mesh with the rest of the group in order to fit in or keep the crew together. While it is wonderful to have loving friends and family, we have to remember to stay true to God and ourselves by revealing on the outside the true person inside of us. Of course not all of your friends will be the same, and I do not encourage you to condemn those who may not be on the same spiritual level because all of us have different vices. Your vice may be sexual dependency, while someone else's vice is gossiping, lying, cheating, or jealousy. We all have fallen short and we have to encourage each other, not condemn one another. Moreover, you should at least know that your true friends would respect and support you no matter what, even if your lives are different. When you assess your friends and the people you are closest to, consider the common values and beliefs you all share, and hopefully the assessment will give you insight into the type of friends you really have.

It is easy to receive advice from people who think they know everything, but have yet experienced anything. For example, why would you ask for marriage advice from someone who has been single all of his or her life? If you were trying to recover from alcohol, drug, or sexual addiction, why would you consult with someone who has never been addicted to anything, including caffeine? Furthermore, if you make a decision your friends have yet to make you could be the one they come to when the time comes for them to experience the same situation you have already overcome. You never know, you could be the catalyst that inspires and encourages your friends to step up and make a change in their lives. In the Bible it teaches us that we overcome through the testimonies of others. If you share your struggles and victories with other people, you could potentially trigger their desire for change living inside of them. This is why it was so important for me to write this book. Understand there will be those who will convince you that you're making the wrong decision because they acknowledge you are raising the standard. They will remind you of how difficult it is and may even try to convince you that it is not worth the sacrifice. No longer will you remain complacent with living your life below your fullest potential, and now others around you will truly reflect on their own lives. They may not be ready to move out of their comfortable state just as you are at that moment. Although you see the benefits of this new change, they may not see it at the same time, but God works in all of us; and, even though their time may not be then, it may come later. It is so awesome how He will work in us to help not only ourselves but also those around us. It is not just about your life changing, but it is about impacting the lives of others. Many times we encourage young people that they are too young to be engaging in sexual activities, but we must reassure ourselves we are living up to the same standards. Moreover, all of us are still babes and children in the life of a Christian, and our lives should reflect growth also.

When you only cared about pleasing yourself and having sex to get that wonderful feeling, whom exactly were you helping? You were not helping anyone, but when you chose to eliminate that part from your life you gained the power to bless so many more than before through your testimony. I could not sit here today and write to you had I not experienced the things I went through, but I knew my struggles could impact the lives of others. No matter what the response, make sure you remain strong with your decision and overcome the pressure of your friends, family, or the enemy.

Is sex that bad?

At this moment, you may be thinking, I'm making too much of the issue when it comes to sex. Well, the truth of the matter is sometimes we don't make a big deal when it comes to sex until later when it is too late. In the beginning when everything seems good we say things like, "Let's do it because I can't wait any longer. I'll pray later and God will forgive me. We'll do it this time, and we'll stop next time." Then something happens that brings tragedy or brings us to our knees and then we say things like, "Lord, please let the pregnancy, STD, AIDS, or even cancer test be negative and I will never have sex again." Another popular statement is, "I can't be pregnant because I'm not ready to have kids." My response is if you are not ready to have kids then you're probably not ready to have sex because that is a risk you take every time you lay down with him, with or without a condom. It appears now that a situation, which we considered only a minute, has turned into something we think is big enough for only God to bring us through. Many of us have been there and have either said and thought the same things. Our fear and anxiety begins to grow within and lasts from as little as 3 minutes or even for weeks or months. You sit there waiting to see if the line will change to two double lines, and deliberate as to how you will be able to work extra hours to support your newborn son/daughter. You sit waiting by the phone to hear the report from the doctor's office praying that you have been spared of gonorrhea, herpes, HPV, or even HIV. You sit and pray wondering if your life will be cut short because of the cancer that could take control over your body. These different situations cause anxiety, stress, and sometimes sickness, and it is not until then when we realize how careless we were with our bodies. We figure now, since we are in a complicated situation that sex is a huge deal because it could have a huge impact on our lives. Instead of choosing to pray later, we should have been praying earlier, "Lord, please give me the strength to overcome this weakness. You are the only one that can deliver me from this." The good news is that God in his goodness and grace will keep us and bless us even during those difficult situations. He brought us through it in victory and even though we may have had to deal with the consequences. He continued to bless us even in the midst of everything. Yes, you conceived a child before marriage or at a young age, but thank God for the beautiful and healthy child you now have.

The only sad thing is as faithful as God is to us, you would think we would try to be faithful to Him. However, even though we pray a prayer of forgiveness in the midst of our situations we soon forget the promise we made to Him, and once again we find ourselves engaged in sexual intercourse. You must consider whether your prayers are aligned with what God would have for you. Re-direct your prayers so that your prayer prevents you from praying the same prayer of repentance every time. If you pray Lord, deliver me and sincerely pray for deliverance from your weakness, then your mind will not have to be troubled with thoughts of unplanned pregnancy or unwanted diseases and/or death. All in all, remember that a moment of passion can cause a lifetime of despair.

The True Meaning of Intimacy

What do we look to gain from omitting sex from the relationship? You gain one of the best qualities for a relationship known as real, true, and deep intimacy. Intimacy can be described as closeness, understanding, and confidence. With real intimacy the closeness is maintained through constant communication between two people who communicate with their hearts and minds and not just with sex. The understanding comes from their ability to respect each other and their opinions, and still be able to discuss things in a way that doesn't promote harmful words or put downs. The confidence comes from knowing that both partners, not just one, are actively pursuing to live a righteous life that is pleasing to God, and can stand strong knowing that they are working together with God. When you are not living consistent with His commandments, then you and your partner cannot begin to truly worship God and develop a relationship with him. Nevertheless, you sit at church holding hands, yet your hearts are not open to hear a word from the Lord because guilt and shame consume your thoughts. You may fake the worship, but you actually lack the confidence in your worship because you do not know if God will really bless you and your partner when you know you are not blessing God. God through his love, mercy, and grace continues, despite our weaknesses, to forgive us and bless us. Even all of us who have been guilty of engaging in sexual immorality can repent and be made whole because of His love toward us.

I experienced true intimacy when I met the love of my life. I will admit I started off making the same mistakes in the beginning and I was treating our relationship just like the old ones I experienced in the past. He was older than me so I was convinced he wanted a woman who would supply his every need including sex. Then, the more we talked and the more time we spent together, the more I realized just how different he was. At that time I couldn't decipher whether it was just my feelings taking control or if he truly was different. There was an aura about him when he spoke to me or interacted with me. He treated me like a real man should treat a real woman, and most importantly, he was a man of God. After spending more time with him, we realized just how much we had prayed for each other. I always knew that God would bless me more than I could ever imagine and I truly realized this once I met him because he was so much more than what I prayed for. We soon realized that God had blessed us with our soul mates. However, I had to check myself very quickly because at the rate we were going we were going to destroy what God had intended for us unless we decided to make a change together. Of course I cannot take the credit for the deliverance that occurred because it was God speaking through my Pastor at that time who pushed me to have the courage to do what was right. All of my life I would hear a message or two about not having sex before marriage, but it wasn't until my recent Pastor did a series on sexual immorality that changed my life. It was the first time I was convicted and at the same time was compelled to really make a change because he would so eloquently and specifically explain how damaging sexual immorality is for us not only physically, but also spiritually. He made us take a closer look as to why sexual immorality was so damaging to our lives, and how it would prevent us from inheriting the Kingdom of God. The disadvantages of sexual immorality were not simply physical but more importantly it affected my spirituality and the future that God had designed for me. Based on everything that was taking place during that time I knew God was about to do a new thing in my life.

So, after weeks of trying but failing and going back and forth, we knew what we had to do. We made the decision to remain abstinent until the day we say I do. I have to admit that at first it seemed like something that was impossible because I was so into him and he was so into me. Naturally, you want to share a physical relationship with someone you are into, and I was definitely attracted to him. His skin is a beautiful milk chocolate with a hint of red tint (he has Cherokee in his blood), his teeth are bright as a pearly white, and his body was strong enough to wrap his manly arms around me and make me feel protected. It was obvious how attracted we were to each other, but we understood that if God was going to bless our union and take us to another level, we also had to go to the next level. Usually, people refer to the next level as sex, but our next level was the level of mature spirituality. We understood how contradictory our prayers would be if we continuously prayed, "Lord, please bless us and keep us together," if we weren't doing the things to receive God's favor. We knew God had brought us together for this special moment and we wanted the moment to last for a lifetime. Nonetheless, our momentary actions were important in shaping the relationship we wanted to last forever.

Worth the wait

Some may be thinking even now, "I just cannot do that. You are better than me because that's just something I'm not strong enough to do." But you know what? I am not better than you or anyone else for that matter. I just want to experience the fullness of God; and, you have to make the same decision if you really want to experience the fullness of God. Some of us have missed out on so many blessings from God because we were not strong enough to say no. Instead of discerning between the good and bad guys, we couldn't because our bodies and minds were filled with so much sin that we couldn't hear from the Lord. We couldn't tell if God was telling us to go right or left on our jobs, in our relationships, and even in our homes. We allowed our flesh and personal desires to influence our actions. Nevertheless, that is when prayer time becomes essential. You have to pray your way through the strong and the weak times. There were times when all we could do was pray because our flesh was trying to control our minds. He even took it a step further and decided that in order to help us remember our promise to God he would purchase a ring to serve as a symbol for our commitment. With our ring we felt empowered and we knew we were serious about our commitment. The ring served as a reminder of our promise and was easily visible even during times of weakness. It has not always been easy for us, but it wasn't easy for Jesus to bear the cross alone either. Nevertheless, Jesus knew everything he endured was worth the sacrifice just to save us and to complete His father's plan, and my soul mate and I felt the same way when it came to this decision. We knew it was worth it because we saw something in each other that we had never seen before. Even as time passes, we find it to be easier and easier. More importantly, God sees something in you that you may not even see in yourself and He wants you to see it in you. He wants you to walk in your destiny and use your womanly qualities in the way it was designed for you.

What seemed to surprise me or took me aback was the fact that the things I experienced in past relationships were not issues for us. The constant paranoia, nagging, or lack of trust was all dismissed because we were experiencing true intimacy—closeness, understanding, and confidence. Ladies, let me tell you. If you have never experienced true intimacy, it is a feeling like no other and I can't wait for you to experience the same. I thanked God all the more because of the fact that He blessed me with someone who did not encourage me to compromise my beliefs and values but challenged me to live a better life. Some of us declared we were going to remain abstinent, but then he came along and we just threw the idea out of the window. However, when you consider someone as a potential mate, each partner should help to inspire and encourage the other to enhance his or her lives. What is the benefit of having a mate if he or she is not a helpmate?

Love vs. Lust

When it comes to experiencing love, we must make sure we do not confuse love with lust. Lust could start off as something that seems natural and innocent because of a cute smile, nice hair, or handsome body, but could ultimately lead to guilt and shame. It is not necessary to include sex in our relationships, but in order to live it is necessary to have a healthy body. We have to consider the consequences of our actions not after the event, but prior to making decisions that could result in a negative outcome. Young ladies, do not fall into the trap of a young boy who pressures you to have sex so you will be his girlfriend. Try to refrain from altering your life plans by engaging in sexual activity because you think you are the only one not having sex. Women, find a man who will accept your beliefs because he too has the same beliefs to prevent him from forcing you to compromise your beliefs. As you grow older, use the wisdom and knowledge you have gained, and learn from your mistakes so you can encourage those ladies who will come after you. Be strong and don't fear making the conscious decision to stand up for what you know is righteous and pure. Your fear will keep you bound and prevent you from going to the next level in your life. Moreover, you will go through life always wondering if things would have been different had you waited or abstained from it. It is my prayer that you will begin to reflect on the consequences that could occur as a result of your decisions and choose wisely in the end. If you consider your decisions for today with open and bright eyes, then your future will not seem as cloudy. You are beautiful and strong, and it is time you quit making excuses for your weakness, and excuse it from your life so in the end you can walk in the fullness of your life.

Reality Speaks: Your actions today will ultimately affect your actions for tomorrow.

Realistic Thinking

Every time I lay down with a different person I feel like:

_____

_____

_____

_____

_____

_____

_____

How many partners have I slept with? What did I gain from sleeping with them?

_____

_____

_____

_____

_____

_____

_____

Out of the people I've slept with, how many of them did I REALLY care about? How did I feel when the relationship ended and why did I feel that way?

_____

_____

_____

_____

_____

_____

Today I commit to changing my "unmarried" sex life by:

_____

_____

_____

_____

_____

_____

Reality Checkpoint #3—Previous "cats" you've dated before make you think of your present one as a dog.

Musiq Soulchild creatively wrote a song known as "Previous Cats" on one of his albums and described the common struggle between a woman, her current boyfriend, and her past relationships. She constantly blamed her new boyfriend for the hurts and pain caused by her past relationships. The new boyfriend has to suffer from the effects of her pain, bitterness, and even low self-esteem even though he did not play a role in her past experiences. Musiq went on to explain that he was not to blame for the hurt and pain caused by what he refers to as her "previous cats" (previous boyfriends). When I first heard this song awhile back, I immediately understood what he was talking about because Musiq Soulchild was talking to me. It was as if he knew exactly what I was feeling and thinking while I was in the relationships. I would say phrases like, "You remind me of my ex. Are you going to lie to me like everyone else did? I do not trust anybody because I have been hurt so many times before." For some, I basically did not give them any chance of proving themselves to me. I just figured the new one would be like the old ones despite my unwillingness to change my thoughts and actions. Since then I have evaluated my past relationships and how they have affected those that proceeded. I was, more times than one, the female who truly and honestly thought all guys were the same. While there are similarities between all men, I learned later in my life that the common denominator in all of my relationships, despite the different men, was in fact ME. I was choosing different men, but still treating them as if they were all the same. There were times when I would begin our very first discussion talking about all (literally all) of the previous guys who hurt me, lied to me, and even cheated on me. When they would ask me to tell them about myself I would immediately provide the specific details about every incident that occurred involving my past experiences with lies and deceit. I would even go as far as explaining every single detail of the incidents. I was trying to move forward but had no idea my heart was located in the past. It was like a therapy session where I would talk, breathe, and release. The only problem was my ex's were merely boyfriends. They were not trained professional psychiatrists.

Of course it is important to know about your partner's past, but we often make the mistake of reflecting on the past a little too much. In our minds, we think if our new guy knows all of the hurt and pain that we've been through in the past, then he will: a. be reluctant to do the same thing, or b. do exactly what was done to us in the past. We linger in the past for too long and cannot let go of what already took place. Basically, ladies, we talk too much sometimes. Every man says it, but I will be the first woman to admit it. Think about it. Have you ever had a friend and every time you call them or ask them how they are doing they always have something to complain about? They talk about how much they hate their job, how their boyfriend is getting on their nerves, how unhappy they are, how they hate looking at themselves in the mirror, or how it is too hot or too cold outside. They always have something bad to talk about. Well, what do you think he thinks when everything you talk about is negative? Yes, you have to talk yourself through difficult situations as a part of therapy, but every conversation does not have to relate to every man in your past who did you wrong. You would not be pleased if he constantly referred to his ex-girlfriends all of the time, so you should show the same courtesy and leave your ex's where they should be, in the past.

Keep it real with yourself

Exit means to have a way out. It is the opposite of entrance, meaning you should not go through an exit to get into something. Moreover, you should not use your ex to go through if you are trying to enter into a new dimension in your life. An experienced driver understands your eyes cannot be focused solely on the rear view mirror, because then you will miss what is ahead of you in the windshield. If you want to keep driving towards success and a better life, quit focusing on the rear view mirror, and pay attention to the windshield of happiness in front of you. In order to keep driving and reach your desired destination, you do in fact have to leave your former location.

In other words, you have to be open and honest with him and yourself. If you find yourself constantly talking about your ex-boyfriends then maybe you have not fully closed the door to your past relationships. Maybe you have unsettled feelings to work out within yourself. When I refer to closing the door, I do not mean going back and forth and leaving the door cracked open for another opportunity, but I truly mean closing the door. Many times we leave the door cracked open just in case he wants to come back through it, and unfortunately this causes us to miss out on the blessings standing right in front of us.

When you finally decide to close that chapter in your life you have to firmly decide in your mind that you want to let go and move on. For instance, quit picking up the phone every time he calls or quit blowing up his phone everyday and claiming that you two are just friends. Clearly, if you two were just friends, you wouldn't feel jealous or sad when he talks about his new girlfriend. You wouldn't think of him in a romantic way when you see or hear him. Quit worrying about what he's doing and forgetting about what you are supposed to be doing. Quit arguing with him all of the time about getting back together, and reminding him of how much he hurt you in the past. If he hurt you and he didn't even apologize, that doesn't mean you need to wait forever for the apology. Nevertheless, you definitely cannot expect your new man to pay for the mistakes your ex made. If you claim to move on but you are still talking about *what used to be* and *what could have been*, then you will never experience *what should be*. You have to be honest with yourself so you will prevent yourself from entering into a new relationship that you are truly not ready to begin. Take time and deal with your feelings. It is okay to say not yet because you are not ready to move on, instead of acting as if everything is okay by covering up your true feelings with new men in your life. You will end up dating different guys with no true feelings for him and wasting time. All of your energy and time will be used to find the better man instead of using the same energy and time to make a better you.

Moving on or staying put?

How do I know if I am treating the new man in my life like one of my previous cats? Sometimes we don't even realize how we are treating our new man until he finally tells us or we look back later in life. It is all in the way you speak and act towards him. If you avoid speaking words of encouragement to him, and replace it with statements that put him down based on situations not related to him, then you may be treating him like a previous cat. For example, you repeatedly tell him he acts just like your ex or you knew he was going to be just like the rest of them. Your words pierce him because you use the words you wanted to say to your ex. You have so much bitterness and anger inside of you that you transfer the same energy towards him as if he is the one causing the pain on the inside. When he tells you how beautiful you are you reply, "Whatever. You probably tell all your "girl" friends the same thing." Another example is when he shares his feelings with you and admits how much he cares for you, but you reply, "Yeah right. Nobody has ever cared about me so why would you care about me". He tells you he wants to take care of you and you reply, "I can do for myself. I do not need you taking care of me. My own daddy didn't even take care of me." All of the replies stem from previous cats that have absolutely nothing to do with your current man. I was guilty of saying this all of the time when I met my soul mate because I was not used to anyone taking care of me and treating me like a Queen. Again, I was caught up in what used to be instead of accepting what should be. Ladies, we must realize that just because our previous guys didn't treat us like we deserved, it does not mean all men want to treat us the same way. Trust, there are some handsome, strong men who are still looking for the real woman so they can treat them like a Queen. We have to make sure, however, that we are the righteous and ready women so the righteous and ready man who was created to be our helpmate will easily identify us.

Of course, you have to discern between real and fake because some men will use trickery and sweet words to get you excited. We have to be careful and make sure we are not naïve into falling for every man who says all the right things. However, when you know he is being genuine and true to you accept it and appreciate his willingness to be a good man. When you resist him you are basically telling him that he cannot do anything for you because you expect him to do what everyone else did. Allow your new man to treat you right and make up for what was missed in your past relationships without making him pay for the mistakes he did not make.

Mr. Wrong vs. Mr. Nice Guy

The funny thing is that sometimes we resist the right things, and accept the wrong things. For instance, we meet a guy who rarely calls, rarely spends time with us, and never keeps his word about anything. For that type of guy we find ourselves bending over backwards and doing everything in our power to make it all work. It may be because he is cute, funny, has a lot of money, or simply because we think he gives us a challenge. We like to refer to the liar, player, and/or womanizer as Mr. Wrong.

Then, here comes another guy who actually pays attention to us, enjoys taking us out, and finds a way to be completely honest and open about everything. He wants to get to know you for you and not for what is in between your legs, and he treats you like a woman should be treated. We refer to him as Mr. Nice Guy who we think sometimes also refer to as Mr. Too Nice. Do not get me wrong, it is important to find someone you are compatible with, but there are times when Mr. Nice is avoided because Mr. Bad is more of a challenge and not too nice. Usually I have noticed Mr. Wrong is the one that all of the girls want to date, so we become extra involved in trying to win him over. We think the chase will be more exciting because out of all the girls we will eventually convince him that he wants to be with us. We make excuse after excuse for Mr. Wrong and still focus our attention on him. So when it is time to have an intellectual conversation with someone else about the future, we find a way for Mr. Wrong to somehow show up as the center of the conversation. Your new guy is getting to know your ex more than you because all you seem to talk about is Mr. Wrong.

I would always focus on Mr. Wrong whether he was present or not because I was so angry with him (or them). I would spend time with other guys hoping that he would find out someway, somehow so he would feel some type of jealousy and ultimately want me back. Sometimes I would plan it just right so that the new guy and my ex's would be at the same place at the same time. I wanted him to feel the hurt and pain I was experiencing and I was using the new guy as a part of my plan. I did not have feelings for the new guy and I was not in a state of mind to allow myself to have feelings for him. It seems pretty childish and immature and that is exactly what it was—childish. I honestly thought his thoughts were consumed with what I was doing, when in reality he was moving on with his life. The interesting fact is that I am not the only one who thinks like that because so many other women actually think the same thoughts. We spend so much time thinking about the ex's and neglect the new men in our lives. It sometimes goes as far as committing the same mistake toward our new guy that was done to us by our previous boyfriends. We figure the transfer of pain (from me to him) will somehow provide healing to the situation we experienced before. This is not true, however, because now we will experience feelings of pain, heartache, guilt and loss because we have ruined a relationship that could have been more than a vengeful incident. Consider the feelings and the potential of your new man, and release the feelings of your past man.

How can I let go of the previous cat so I avoid treating my new man like a dog?

The first thing you must do is just that—you must let go. I mentioned earlier how you must close the door to that chapter in your life and start a whole new book. You have to be open and honest with yourself and decide if you are truly ready to move on. If there are things you and your ex need to sort through then you handle your business, but do not allow it to linger on for so long that your life remains stagnant in that same place for years to come. If he's been talking about you two getting back together for months or even years, then you just have to accept reality and know that most likely it will not happen. His actions should coincide with his words.

You must also be honest with your new guy and let things flow. Some times we do not plan to meet Mr. Nice Guy and we neglect to be honest about our feelings in fear of not ever meeting anyone else like him. However, you have to be honest about your feelings so both of you will know how slow or fast to take the relationship in order to prevent one's feelings from being hurt. If you are honest with him and explain how you need more time or how you want to move on, but just at a slower pace, then you two will have an understanding, a strong friendship could be established, and he may even be able to help you work through the pain.

Forgiveness, which may seem impossible, must also take place in order to sincerely avoid potential harm toward your new man. Forgiveness is very difficult for many, but is very necessary in the process of healing through all of the past relationships. Forgiveness is the fire starter that ignites the healing process. We cannot begin to fully heal from our past if we cannot fully forgive those who hurt us. Of course our minds may not help us to forget the situations entirely, but the forgiveness will bring a peace over our hearts and minds when we have those low moments and begin to reflect on the hurt and pain we experienced. Most of the time the bitterness and the anger we exhibit within our new relationships stems from our unwillingness to forgive. Forgiveness takes place when you are able to excuse his actions and pardon his behavior. Trust when I say I know firsthand how difficult it is to forgive others who have wronged you.

It was some years ago when I learned first hand how forgiveness plays an integral role in the process of healing. I was confronted by a good friend, Paula, who wanted to come out with some truth about a past friend of mine, Tasha. Paula sat me down and immediately my heart began racing because I knew she was not about to bring some bad news. She proceeded to tell me how my relationship with Tasha was built on nothing but lies. I soon found out that Tasha had been with almost every man I had ever dated in the past. While I was being the best friend I could be she was living a life of deceit because she was not being honest with me about any of this. Of course, some of the pain would not have been so detrimental if sex had not played a role in any of the relationships, but I had to face reality. She shared something with someone else that I thought was special between my ex and me. A situation occurred when she betrayed me the most when she engaged in sexual relations with one of my ex-boyfriends I had been with for awhile and all the while she acted as if nothing happened. Please understand that all of these events occurred while I was actually in the relationship. It was not even until years later when I found out exactly what happened. My friends did not approve of our friendship, but I never understood why. Their disapproval stemmed from the fact she was not being honest with me and hadn't been for years. So, for years I shared my deepest secrets, time, and love with a friend who was using me to get closer to him. Maybe you too have experienced betrayal by a good friend or an ex, but know that you too can heal even if it takes some time.

I will admit, at first, I felt a rage rise up in my spirit because I was so hurt and could not believe that a so-called "best friend" would do something so hurtful. I cannot even elaborate as to the details of everything I found out during the entire process, but it was enough to make you not want to trust anybody ever again in life. I was ready to confront her and I was even ready to fight. Yes, I was ready to fight because the flesh was taking over my mind and spirit and I figured that was the only way for me to release my anger. Ladies, you know how it gets sometimes when we just want to settle by fighting. We have to make sure, however, that we don't always react based on our first instincts.

Furthermore, I attempted to confront her and ask her if any of this was true and there she stood cursing at me and accusing me of lying. Wow! Her reaction reflected what I thought my reaction should be. I was at a boiling point, but thankfully we parted ways at that moment in order to avoid further physical altercation. Later that evening, more and more truths were being revealed about the one whom I had called my best friend for some time now. By then I was convinced that I was going to go to her place, find her, and fight until I got tired. Coincidently, it was Wednesday night and I decided I would go to church for Bible study instead because it was part of the weekly routine. One of my friends did her best to calm me down to prevent me from doing something I would regret. So, I decided to go and clearly the Lord was speaking right to me. My pastor at the time was teaching a message dealing with something I needed to know more about right at that time—forgiveness. Can you believe it? The last thing I wanted to hear about at that moment was the actual message I needed to hear at that moment. The Pastor was explaining to us how important it is to forgive and why it is so critical for our healing process. He reminded us that God forgives us everyday despite our iniquities. All I could do was cry because I knew God was speaking through my Pastor and directly to me. He knew how hurt I was, but even in that moment He gave me what I needed the most—his love and comfort. God has a funny way of showing up in our time of need. Even when we don't think we need something only He knows what's best for us. I sat there contemplating how different the situation would have been if I had followed my first instinct. Basically, I would have missed the opportunity to hear from God and do the right thing.

Once the tears finally dried up, I knew what I had to do. We had the opportunity to meet up and again, ironically at church, and discussed the allegations and rumors alone without any disruptions or public viewing. She finally admitted her actions and confessed most of the things that were told to me. Although my flesh still wanted to harm her in some way, I remembered the lesson from the past Wednesday and simply replied, "I'm hurt and I do not like it, but I forgive you." What? I didn't fight her? I didn't curse her? No, because by then I realized that my forgiveness and my reactions right then and there would affect my future relationships and future dealings with people who would hurt me. She was not the first person who hurt me, although it was one of the most painful experiences, and she definitely was not going to be the last. If I had chosen not to forgive her, then I would have talked about that situation in every single relationship forever. The forgiveness allowed me to accept what happened and move on. I had to excuse both his and her actions and find a way to deal with my personal pain. It was difficult to forget, but the forgiveness granted me serenity over the raging and angry feelings inside. I felt good because I allowed God to dictate my actions instead of choosing to handle the situation my own way.

The same thing can and could occur with you and your past relationships. You have to forgive him. Yes, he cheated on you with your best friend, he cheated on you and impregnated another woman, he lied to you and said he did not have kids, he lied and said he was not married, he lied and said you were his one and only, he lied and said he wanted to marry you, or he left you for someone else you would least expect. All of the situations occurred in the past and that is exactly where you must leave it because you do not want to blame your current guy for your previous guys' mistakes. Regardless of the hurt and pain you experienced, you have to forgive him because your resentment and despair will just continue over into your next relationship. Because I forgave him and her, I could go on with my life and avoid having to make my present man suffer because of my past sufferings. I did not have to throw it up in his face all of the time and act as if he was the cause for my pain. I acknowledged those involved in the scandal, turned my negative energy into positive energy and refused to let the situation dictate my entire life.

Broken heart

I know how difficult it is to mend a broken heart, but I had to resist the desires to be vengeful and coldhearted, and instead I surrendered to God and asked Him to help heal my broken heart. Many times we go from one guy to the next thinking the next man will heal us from our past pains, when in actuality it is only Him above that can mend our broken hearts. Your bitterness, anger, and callous feelings will make you so unattractive because no man, or anyone for that matter, wants to be around someone who is always upset and down because of things that took place days, weeks, months, or even years ago. Reject the bitterness inside of you because otherwise the bitterness will take control over your entire mind, body, and soul. Your facial expressions and body language will exhibit disgust and in your soul you will feel empty and cold. Moreover, you will resist the love and compassion from anyone who even tries to make things better because you will place a wall up to prevent anyone from coming near you. Of course we must guard our hearts, but our actions should still reflect a caring and warm spirit that lives inside of us. You know it lives inside of you, but you have to waken the spirit within you through prayer and submission to God's strength and power. Energy is neither lost nor destroyed;

rather it is transferred (as described by Newton's laws). Therefore, the same energy you use to support your anger, sadness, and bitterness is the same energy you can transfer to bring about peace, love, and forgiveness.

Reality Speaks: No one carries his or her luggage around all of the time; so, unpack your baggage and quit carrying your dead weight!

Realistic Thinking

Circle the response that closely matches what you would say or do.

When someone asks me about my past relationships I respond by:
  a. Highlighting significant experiences, and discussing what I learned from them.
  b. Explaining every intricate detail of every relationship I've ever experienced.
  c. Discussing every bad thing that men have ever done to me, and explaining how they ruined every relationship.

When my partner tries to do nice things for me, I respond by:
  a. Saying "Thank You" and showing my appreciation.
  b. Ignore the gesture because I really don't expect him to be so nice anyway.
  c. Questioning why he's being so nice and accusing him of being guilty for some reason.

When my partner says, "You can trust me" and acts accordingly, I respond by saying:
  a. "I know I can trust you. You've never given me a reason not to trust you."
  b. "I guess I trust you. I trust you to do what you're going to do."
  c. "Trust you? Yeah right. I don't trust any man especially after what I've been through.

When my partner makes an honest mistake and apologizes for it, I respond by:
  a. Discussing the situation and accepting his apology.
  b. Ignoring the situation as if it never happened.
  c. Telling him, "You're just like every other man because you're always messing up."

After dating for several months, my partner decides he wants to become exclusive. He asks me to be his girlfriend and I respond most likely by saying:
  a. "Why not? As long as we talk about our expectations, we're both on the same level, and can communicate and be honest, then I don't have a problem."

    b. "I don't know if I'm ready."

    c. "I would, but I don't want to be with anyone ever again because I've been hurt so bad in the past. You would hurt me too. I know you would."

Findings based on your responses:

Mostly A's	You are with dating without focusing all of your attention on your past relationships. You do not feel the need to carry the baggage into your relationship, and you are comfortable with discussing situations without sounding bitter.
Mostly B's	You are somewhat ready to move on, but you are still hesitant. You play the role as if you are ready to move on, but deep down inside you keep wondering if you really are. In your mind you think he's going to mess up or he will treat you like your ex's treated you. If his words are aligned with his actions, embrace it and move on.
Mostly C's	It is obvious that you are still carrying all of your baggage. You are still dealing with the hurt and pain from your past relationships, and now you are causing him to carry your load. You expect him to clean up the mess your ex's left behind. Take time to deal with your feelings so he can feel admiration instead of animosity.

Reality Checkpoint #4—You think of him as a piece of clay that you will be able to mold into what you want him to be.

It is an amazing thing to sit and watch a potter mold his dull and messy clay into a beautiful piece of art. It starts off looking like a muddy mess, and turns into a wonderful pot, glass, plate, or whatever the potter chooses to design. We place the finished product in our homes, in our living rooms, or on display shelves as an exhibit for others to see. The potter of course did not design the clay but he/she puts great effort into creating a piece of work that they will be pleased with in the end and for others to enjoy. Some consider this a hobby and some even make a career out of creating these items. The potter, however, is working with clay and not humans, so it is unrealistic to think we can do the same thing with people, in particular men. Some times we think we can mold men into what we want them to be by trying to make them what we want we them to be. I have been guilty of this and I've seen it done so many times before. We get so set into thinking that we can change him, but if someone was trying to change you would you really be cooperative with the idea? You would probably say, "This is me and this is how I will be forever. No one can change me." So, I ask, why are we trying to do the same thing with men? Changing our hair, clothes, or any other outward appearance is easier than changing what is on the inside. Think about yourself. If someone came to you and asked you to change your outfit, the proposition would probably be fairly easy, but if someone asked you to change your attitude or your personality, then it wouldn't necessarily be so easy to do at that moment. This would take time to change the person inside of you because you have lived with you your entire life. You would probably be reluctant to even try because you want to hold onto your self-identity. When I used to teach in the classroom I remember how difficult it was to change the students' way of thinking. I would try to get them to envision a better future, but they did not understand because they were already molded into the type of people they wanted to be based on their environment and how they were raised. I knew I had the power to influence their thoughts and behavior, but ultimately they would have to make the change on their own. Change is a really good thing especially when it is a change for the better and when the person realizes the need for a change. However, when we try to force change on others to cater to what we want or think we need, then we are not interested in change for the better; rather we are interested in change for personal gratification—change for me. Think about when you minister or are ministered to about your spirituality. No one wants you to force them to come to church, and force them to make a change; instead a nice invitation or sharing of the good news and your personal testimony is more effective because the focus is less on you and more on what God has done in your life. The same is true when you meet your man. Reality check, Ladies: You cannot force him to do something he does not want to do.

Baby Mama Drama

I have been guilty of it before and have seen it so many times. We meet this guy and are immediately attracted to him, but later realize that he may not be compatible with who we really are, so we do one of two things: a. cater to how he is and become more like him, or b. try to change who he is so that he will be more like us. The first choice is just as damaging as the second one because ultimately we change who we really are. The second choice shows how controlling or desperate we may be because we will go through anything just to make sure he is more like us or better imaged as someone who we are really looking for. Instead of accepting the fact that we are just too different and should only be friends, we ignore the feelings in fear of never being able to meet someone as fine or fun as he is.

Think of the young lady who meets a gentleman who seems so great until she realizes he has kids and even some "baby mama drama." I am talking about those who really have baby mama drama because they are not taking care of the kids, or he continuously argues with his children's mother but refuses to let her go. She convinces herself that she will be first in his life and that the baby mama drama is something she can ignore. So, she decides to try and change how much time he spends with his kids and his feelings toward his children's mothers. She finds ways to act jealous and cruel to him accusing him of not spending enough time with her. She tries to change his opinions of his children's mothers, his attitude toward his children, or even tries to change the entire situation by declaring that she wants to have kids by him too. The only contradiction is that you knew he had kids to begin with and you knew how close he and his "baby mama" were, but now you want to try and change everything. You are trying to mold him into a man who spends all of his time pleasing you. You are not concerned with his children or his children's mothers for that matter.

There are men who take care of their responsibility regardless of the situation because they are examples of good men. You have to let a man be a man and take care of his responsibilities. You cannot waste time trying to change his mind about that and what he has grown accustomed to doing—taking care of his kids. If he is being honest and showing you that he cares about you and his children and you really want to be with him, then instead of changing him you need to change you. You have to change your attitude and realize that it is not all about you. You will have to change your speech by talking positively about the children and her. Your actions will need to change because you cannot just fall out and throw a tantrum when he wants to spend more time with his kids. Lastly, your heart must change in order to share your love for him with those whom he cares about. If you claim to love him, then you must love everything about him and appreciate his willingness to change his selfish attitude in order to cater more to his children.

Then you have the female who tries to have his baby because she thinks it will change their relationship and make him love her more. The only problem is she knows in the beginning that his other "baby mama" loves drama and she will have no other girl trying to take him, but you still think you will be able to change him and the situation. It becomes a competition between you and the other children's mothers because you think it will work if you just have another child by him. You thought he would want you more and he would change his life because you were going to give him the little girl or boy he always wanted. However, once he finds out you are expecting a little one he begins acting what you think is different and he begins to ignore your phone calls or the arguments begin everyday. You start thinking he has changed and he is not what he used to be, but truthfully he is the same he has always been. You just ignored how he interacted with the other mother because you thought you would be the one to change him. You begin to feel hurt and pain because you feel like he is rejecting you when in actuality you rejected yourself to begin with by focusing mainly on him and what he needed to change. Now you have to deal with the reality of knowing that you assumed you had the power to change something you could not change. You have to make the decision, however, to either deal with the issue and respect him as your loving and compassionate man, or say goodbye to him if he is playing games and trying to be with you and all of his "baby mamas." No matter what the situation, make the best decision that will bring about the least amount of drama.

Defeat the Cheat within Him

When it comes to the cheating men in our lives, those are the ones we think we can definitely change. We see him in the club, on campus, at work, at a lounge and he is so debonair in the way he looks, walks, and talks. He is the hot man on campus or the hunk at work, or the flashy one at the lounge that every woman wants to get close to—in more ways than one. He is also known as the habitual cheater because he chooses one special lady and decides to add a few extra women to his repertoire. You may have known his ex-wife/girlfriend or you may even know his current girlfriend or wife. Regardless of his current situation, you decide you have everything in your power to change his cheating ways. You think because you are so beautiful, your smile is so captivating, your heart loves so much, your personality is so rare, and even your bedroom skills are so great that there is no way he will cheat on you. So, you begin your quest in hopes of changing his actions and his mindset. You make it a point to be with him, despite the fact that he may already be taken, and you even do your best to remain faithful and honest to him. Things seem to be going well, and you even think he will eventually leave the other women alone. Then, you notice his cell phone is constantly ringing or buzzing from calls and text messages from random women. He only acknowledges you in the privacy of his or your home. He refuses to let you meet his female friends or avoids the situation whenever you bring up the topic. You hear random rumors from your close friends about how he was hugging and sitting close with different women at random places. Clue after clue tells you that something is not right, but you still hold on to the fact that you will cause the great change in his life. You force him to come to church and pray that the Pastor will speak a word to him about being faithful, or you bring him around other married couples so he will magically gain the "faithful spirit" which will cause him to change his ways. You know deep down inside he is cheating, but you play the naïve role, and ignore the female intuition screaming within your soul. Some women do not ignore their intuition; rather they accept the cheating and continue in the relationship anyway.

Finally, the truth is revealed and your worst fears are made known. You find out he has been cheating the entire time. Surprise! Yes, you should be surprised not because he cheated but because you actually thought he was going to change just because you were in his life and forcing him to change. Any man I know that has turned from his playing ways to become a faithful man did it because deep down inside that is what he wanted and he only did it when they were ready. Although there may have been a woman to help inspire the change, it was only by his personal decision that the change took place. What makes us think that we are so great that we can change anybody? If you knew he was cheating and acting a mess when you first united with him, what makes you think he will be faithful to you? Immediately the relationship started with lies and deceit, and yet you thought the trust would magically appear from nowhere. Anyone can talk a good game and claim they are not going to cheat, but the proof is in their actions. You have to be willing to put your foot down and let them know you are not putting up with that mess. Otherwise, you will find yourself sharing your man. I am all about forgiveness and second chances, but you have to know what you are going to put up with. Tyler Perry made it known in one of his great plays that you can let a man make a mistake, but just don't let him keep making the same mistake over and over again. Repent means to turn away and change your ways. Just because he keeps telling you he is sorry, does not necessarily mean just that if he continues doing the same thing. It is like putting your hand in a fire. If you put your hand in the fire and it burns you, will you put your hand in there again? Moreover, will you attempt to change the fire into a liquid when you do not have the skills to do so? Do not waste time trying to change him, but instead change the relationship by changing whom you choose to be with.

Red means Stop, Green means Go—Pay Attention to the signs

During one of my first relationships, I remember the first day my ex-boyfriend and I decided to make it official, a young lady called me. She heard that he and I were starting our relationship and wanted to warn me. She explained to me that he had tried to pursue her for the past few weeks—the same few weeks we were supposedly dating. She even agreed to call him on three-way to see if he would mention me as his new girlfriend. So, doing it the old school way, we decided to call him on three-way and I let her do all of the talking. She asked him about their hook up and if he would come over to her house, and he played right into it by suggesting they hook up. I could not believe it. This was the same day we decided to make it official and now I had to hear all of this! He did not mention my name once during the conversation. So, why did

I end up being with him for more than a few years despite the information I had obtained in the beginning? I'll tell you why. I thought I could change him and make him want to be with me. The first incident was not the only one because the rumors and lies continued all throughout our relationship, but I was comfortable with him and did want to see him with anyone else. I thought I would change his way of thinking and I thought he would just get tired of the girls and want to change his actions. I even went as far as to think that the other girls were minor compared to me because at the end of the day he was coming home to me. Yeah, he was coming home to me, but by the end of the day he had already been with at least 2 or 3 other girls. We say things like this all of the time to justify our number 1 spot, but who really and truly wants to share their man with another woman? We are worth more than just a name added to his list of "play pals." If I had realized that I could not change his ways in the beginning then I would have eliminated quite a bit of hurt and pain I experienced later in the relationship.

You can't change the abuser, but you can change the abuse.

Physical abuse is sometimes a part of the relationship that we think we will be able to change also. There are times even in the beginning when the signs are clear. He always wants to know your every move and calls to make sure you are where you say you are. He tries to control how you feel and what you do. At first we think it is cute because we think he is so into us, and cares about us so much. Reality check, Ladies: He is more into controlling what we do. He may even grab you and throw you up against the wall and explain later how much he loves you, but reminds you that you cannot make him that upset. You become brainwashed into thinking what he says is actually true. So, if you want to abuse to stop, you must make it stop. If you can't change the abuser, change the abuse by getting rid of it.

Yet and still, in the midst of everything, we decide that our actions will change his actions. We conclude that if we allow him to say and do whatever he can to us, then he will eventually stop because he will see how much we are trying to do better. The only problem is that we are doing all of the changing and encouraging his behavior. He will not change because a man will continue doing what you allow him to do. Why would he change his ways if you are fine with it and you do not stand up to his abuse? The abuse only stops when you turn from it and make him realize that you will not accept his behavior. Although his actions may not change instantly, your life will change from being a victim of his abuse to becoming a victor over his abuse.

There are times when we even think our man will change his beliefs and decide to become a part of our religion or worship in the same way we do. In the beginning you have the discussion about spirituality and your beliefs and quickly notice how different you two are. You try to force your beliefs on him thinking that you will change his life and change his mind. Sharing the good news and forcing the good news are two totally different things. It is our responsibility to share our values and beliefs, but you cannot try to change him just so he will be more like you. Your motives behind the change are completely incorrect, especially if you know you two do not see eye-to-eye at all when the issue of religion is brought up. Again, you are trying to change a part of him that has been in his life for a long time. If you two are sincerely seeking oneness in your relationship then it is possible for him to make a change, but not if there is a constant struggle between whose religion is better. You can definitely influence others to believe based on your personal testimony and witness. However, if your life contradicts what you say, then no one—including your man—will want to believe.

Change those things that you have the power to change

Change refers to transformation or modification. When I think of change I think of an addict trying to recover from alcohol, drugs, nicotine, or even sexual dependency. No matter how much you try to convince them to get help, they cannot change until they make the decision. One of the first steps for the addict is to acknowledge they have a problem and decide that they want to get help and want to make a change. The same thing is true for anyone who is not an addict. You cannot force someone to change but the person has to decide that a change is necessary. Simply put, if he was like that in the beginning then most likely he will be like that until he wants to change and not when you decide to change him. You cannot be upset with him just because you chose to put up with his mess or his personality that you knew you would not like. Even when it was time for you to grow and change you did it on your own time. There may have been times when people thought or told you it was time for a change but you refused until you were ready. They have to want a better life for themselves. You may call him a womanizer, an habitual liar, a horrible person, a dog, a bad example of a man, a man with no morals and values, or just worthless.

Nonetheless, the longer you put up with him, the more you will give him a reason to act the same way. Your decision to stay, despite the mess, influences his decision to stay and continue doing what he has always done. There is something to be said about a woman who will stand up and refuse to accept the games, the lies, and the mistreatment. I like to refer to her as an EW—Empowered Woman. She is empowered because she takes authority over her life and out of his hands. She no longer allows her man to control her actions; she, instead, is made powerful through her strength and confidence. Today, claim your position as an EW and claim authority, through God's power, over your life. If you realize he is not the man you need to be with, then accept it and move on. You do not have to lower your standards and have a false reality of thinking he will change just for you. Think back to the men you have dated and consider who did most of the changing or initiated change in the other person. Unfortunately, it may have been you, but you can still find the real you and decide to change only those things you can change.

There is a simple prayer I have heard time and time again which says, "Lord, please grant me the serenity to accept those things I cannot change, the courage to change the things I can, and the wisdom to know the difference." This is the reality of it all ladies. If we can sincerely pray this pray and acknowledge that we have no power to truly change someone else, our lives will accept the plans God has designed specifically for our lives. When you accept things you cannot change, you must deal with situations and people by which you cannot control. You have to face reality and realize that there will be things you will not be able to change. Gain courage to actually make changes when you can. For instance, if you can change your relationship by stepping out of it, do not let fear consume your thoughts and prevent you from making wise decisions. When we meet the guy who actually is a good match for us, despite his strengths and weaknesses, we have to accept the good and the bad. Or if the guy is clearly not a good match for us then we have to be bold enough to change what we can in the relationship, and usually we cannot change the person; rather we can change our status and role in the relationship by removing ourselves from the situation, or improving ourselves. Sometimes, it may just come down to a simple compromise being made where both partners need to change their ways. You just have to know how to discern whether the situation should change, or if someone should change. The difference is very important to recognize because you do not want to waste time trying to change things you do not have control over when all the while you missed the opportunity to change what was most important—you.

Reality Speaks: You may need to change your role in the situation, instead of trying to change the other person.

Realistic Thinking

What are some things you've dealt with in your past relationships that you thought would change, but never did?

_____
_____
_____
_____
_____
_____
_____
_____
_____
_____

How long did you wait before a change occurred? Was it worth the wait?

_____
_____
_____
_____
_____
_____
_____
_____
_____

As far as improving myself, I feel I could change/improve my:

_____
_____
_____
_____
_____
_____
_____
_____
_____

Reality Checkpoint #5—Trying to keep up with the Joneses— also known as your girlfriends.

"Girlfriends" is one of my favorite television shows because it really shows the dynamics of relationships we have with our girlfriends. All of the girls—Joan, Lynn, Toni (old shows), and Mya—are unique in their own way through their personalities, characters, and even values. Although they are different, usually they all have one thing in common—men. One may be starting a new relationship, getting re-married, dating different men, or even getting a divorce. They each share secrets and opinions and even occasionally argue with each other. I remember when Joan was so jealous of Toni because she was getting married and Joan was on the brinks of disaster with Ellis. She thought if Toni was getting married she should have been married by then also. I felt like "Girlfriends" was one of the first shows that really showed the interactions and workings of women and their best friends.

I love my girlfriends with all of my heart and consider them as my sisters. We, and I'm sure your girlfriends also, talk about everything, and some of course you are closer to others more than some, but all in all you remain girlfriends. Through good times and bad times your girlfriends provide guidance and advice, whether good or bad, or even just a listening ear. We share secrets and dreams with each other. We hang out and swap stories. We pledge sororities and graduate from college together. We go out and have a good time and even scope the scene for men together. All in all our girlfriends play an integral role in our lives because they learn and understand who we are, how we dress, how we think, how we talk and what we tend to do because a vast amount of our time is spent with each other. There are even times when we know each other better than we are willing to admit to ourselves.

We all love our girlfriends, but sometimes we allow our girlfriends to dictate too many areas of our lives whether at home, on our jobs, at school, or even in our relationships. We go to them about things just because they are our girlfriends and not because they are experts for that type of situation. We make decisions based on what we think they would do or would say instead of considering what is best for our lives. For instance, think about a woman who is involved in a relationship, but repeatedly asks for advice from the girlfriend who has never been in a relationship. Although you can learn from other's mistakes, you may not be the best person to give advice about relationships. This is not to say some cannot learn merely by observation, but a married woman would most likely receive the advice from another married woman because they share the same experience. So many times we have a situation dealing with our boyfriends and immediately we tell our girlfriends. We tell our girlfriends in order to justify our argument or what we think is right. We go from the beginning to end explaining each intricate part of the argument. Think about the number of times you have told your girlfriends about your disagreements, or how he made you upset about something he did? If you are telling your girlfriends all of the bad things and trying to find justification for your actions, then what type of image are you creating for them? It is okay to talk to your girls about your situations but you should not have to check in with them every time a problem occurs. For example, a situation may occur and you may think about talking it out with you boyfriend, but then your girlfriends convince you to ignore him and wait for him to come around. Now, it becomes a battle of the sexes and a game only immature people would play. Your friends convince you to keep him waiting by the phone when you know deep down inside you want to work things out and be the bigger person. Moreover, you find yourself caught in the middle of a war between your girlfriends and your man because he thinks they are out to get him and your girlfriends think he is out to get them. In order to avoid risking your relationship and your friends, you have to discern what to tell your friends and what you should simply keep between you and your man.

Do not be afraid of the truth

I remember when I was in college and one of my friends was dating this new guy. Frequently, she would share stories about how bad he was treating her and how she thought he was lying to her about different things. I even noticed how he treated her in public, and how he refused to acknowledge her. Whenever she found time to talk to me, it was always about how horrible he was treating her. Week after week it was something new until finally I realized that if he was that bad then he was not worth the time or the effort. So, I ended up telling her exactly how I felt in our conversation. She was talking about him and how she did not know what to think about their relationship. I explained to her that I did not want her with someone who was making her upset all of the time. I told her I thought she was worth more than how he was treating her, and he was not worth the time. I truly felt that way not because I was jealous or anything, but because I wanted her to be happy. The next day after our long conversation, I was approached by none other than her boyfriend. He confronted and questioned me about the comments I made and why I felt he was not right for her. He knew every detail about the conversation. What I thought was a private conversation between two girlfriends turned out to be a public announcement. I could not believe she told him everything we discussed. I had to let him know plain and simple why I said the things I did, but then again I should have known she was going to tell him. I explained to him how she was constantly telling me stories about him and how bad he treated her. Of course he was offended because she neglected to tell me about the good things that were going on in their relationship. Now, I was caught in the middle of a relationship where I did not belong and all because my friend was trying to get advice from too many sources. My recommendations would have been completely different had I known more about the good aspects of their relationships. Nevertheless, I could only make a conclusion based on the information I was told. I learned my lesson quickly. I knew then that in the future I would weigh the pros and cons prior to making a decision as to what my girlfriends should do, and I would not be so quick to make a judgment because sometimes people just have hard times in relationships. In my own relationships I stopped telling my girlfriends only the pessimistic aspects of my relationship in order to avoid another situation like this one.

As girlfriends, we can be somewhat complicated. We are so quick to give the best advice but so reluctant to take our own advice. I have seen it time and time again. "Girl, if that was me I would not put up with that. I would kick him to the curb." The "it" could refer to cheating, disrespect, or abuse, and no matter what it is we think we have the answer to every problem. Well, where is this strong and independent power when your man does the same thing? When you know he is cheating or constantly beating you, why aren't you giving yourself the same advice? Moreover, what you think you would do may not be the best advice for someone else to do. You know the right and smart thing to do, but when it comes to applying the advice you find it difficult to do that. Your girlfriends whether you know it or not are tired of it too because you are so quick to give them counsel about their relationships, but refuse to listen to yourself. By reading this book you've probably heard things you have told yourself before but just never applied it. Reality check: I want you to start using the same advice you voluntarily give to your girlfriends, and start applying it to your own life. Otherwise, your words will contradict your actions, and your credibility will be lost. No longer will you be considered a strong woman, but instead you will be considered a weak woman resisting wise advice. The previous chapter reflected on changing those things we can control, so if you know you cannot control your girlfriends actions then control the ones you can—your actions.

What God has for me, it is for me.

When a man/woman has a suit/dress tailored, it is tailored to fit each individual based on his or her weight, height, and measurements. Your size may not be suitable for someone who is smaller or larger than you. The same is true when we consider how God designs our lives—tailored to fit each and every one of us specifically. At times we allow our girlfriends' actions to dictate our actions because we think we have to do what they do. If they are single then we want to be single. If they are in a relationship we feel like we should be in a relationship. Just because they are in a relationship and you are single does not mean you have to feel like you are not a part of the crew. You will find yourself staying in a lifeless relationship that does not add any value to your life just to make sure you fit in with the Joneses—your girlfriends. What about what you need? You cannot always go with the masses just to fit in. Even though you and your girlfriends are similar in so many ways, you still have to be an individual. You have to acknowledge that your lives will be different because God has a unique plan for every one of us.

Besides comparing our relationship status to one another, we find ourselves comparing our men to our girlfriends' boyfriends because we think their standards should be our standards. Johnny buys her a ring so you think you need a ring. Johnny buys her clothes all of the time so you want clothes all of the time. Johnny spends every waking moment with her so you want your man to spend every waking moment with you. Reality check: their standards do not have to be your standards. Your girlfriend prefers a man who plays sports and is in the entertainment business, but you prefer a man who is involved with corporate America and chooses to wear a suit instead of a football uniform. You are not wrong for wanting different things. I'm sure you and your girlfriends have a different sense of style or preference when it comes to clothing and food, so most likely you will have a different preference when it comes to men also. The commonality between all of your boyfriends should, however, include honesty, loyalty, and communication—all of which are important to any type of relationship. All in all, be you and do you in only the way only you know how.

Sometimes jealousy will seep into the minds of our girlfriends or even ourselves, and we will find a way to be negative about the relationship in hopes of the relationship ending. Some girlfriends are even known to covet your man and try to get with them, but hopefully you are not that type. They will try to "hate" (look with disgust) on your relationship because of the quality time you and your man spend with each other, and they may even convince you to spend less time with him and more time with them. Then, you, feeling as if your girlfriends are always right decide to neglect your boyfriend in order to please your girlfriends. There has to be a healthy balance between the time you spend with your man and the time you spend with your friends because both are important in your lives. Nevertheless, "misery loves company" so you have to be careful and make sure your girlfriends are not trying to make you as miserable as they are because they do not have a man. I have seen so many relationships ruined because the girlfriends were always feeding bad advice into the girlfriend simply because they could not stand the thought of someone else being happy. The same girlfriend you caught or found out was cheating with your man, is the same girlfriend who envies your life. She wants what you have and is willing to go to any limit to say that she has the same thing. Be careful though because she is the same girlfriend who really needs to love herself more and needs to know that her life does not have to be like everyone else's.

Which one are you—the girl who envies others or the one she envies? No matter what remember to congratulate your girlfriend on her happiness and do not spoil the fun. Embrace her new man as part of your extended family because eventually he may become a part of the family. Tell her how happy you are for her and find joy even in her blessings. Do not act fake about it, but encourage her and help her through the good and the bad times. Just because they may experience problems does not mean it opens the door for you to automatically suggest a break-up. Provide good, sound advice that will help her and could ultimately help you in your future relationships. As women, we have to find it in ourselves to encourage each other. Your girlfriend really cares about your opinions and how you feel about her new man, but if all you can say is, "Well, just make sure he is not cheating on you like everybody else," then you are not being as positive as you should be. You should be able to celebrate in her happiness when it is truly sincere and real, and even if you know she may be making the wrong decision.

On the other hand, women, sometimes you need to listen to your girl-friends because they may be trying to help you or prevent you from get-ting hurt. Sometimes your girlfriends see you going through the same situation they experienced in the past, and can really give you insight on what you need to do to overcome the situation. There are times when your girlfriends will see so much more than you because they are looking from the outside. Our pride and dependency keeps us from examining our relationship based on the instruction we receive from our girlfriends. We are prideful in thinking that she has no idea what she is talking about or we assume she is just jealous. It is hard to see the damaging effects of your actions when you are in the midst of the situation. Sometimes we are blinded by what we think is love or just simply the lust because we are caught up in the moment. Our dependency comes from our yearning and desire to be with a man so we ignore their womanly advice in order to keep what we think belongs to us. You have either been the woman who: tried to give advice, refused the advice, or you were a combination of both. I have been on both sides of the fence and in the end I always look back and acknowledge those times when I should have listened in the first place.

During one of my troubled relationships, my friends warned me about my boyfriend and explained how they were almost 100% sure he was lying to me about some things. I ignored their assumptions at first because I was convinced they did not want me to be happy. They were just jealous because I had a "good man" and they did not, so I thought. I was so wrong because my girlfriends were actually right about every-thing. I basically chose him over my girlfriends because I wanted to please him more than anything. Even though their information seemed valid and substantial I pretty much ignored the accusations. Eventually, the truth was brought to light and they were in fact telling the truth about everything. How embarrassed did I feel when I realized how wrong I was? The same girlfriends that I pushed to the side for that moment were the same girlfriends who encouraged me during and even after the breakup. They were the same girlfriends who used even a simple letter to remind me of how beautiful I was and to tell me how much I deserved only the best. They were the same friends who encouraged me even in the midst of my lowest moments. This goes to show that usually your true girlfriends want what is best for you and they honestly do not want to see you hurt or in pain. I know my girls wanted the best for me because even when they met my soul mate they saw something special in him before I wanted to admit it. How did they know? Well, when your closest or best friends know you, they pretty much have a good idea of the type of person you should be with, and they only the best for you.

Ladies, ignore the pride and listen to what she is telling you; and, if you are the girlfriend that knows something does not appear right then go to your friend with a calm and courageous spirit even if you have to tell her about the mistakes she is making. As girlfriends we cannot expect to be a part of every aspect of the relationship and try to be in the middle of everything; rather we must provide love and support when they want to listen and even when they do not want to listen, but in a respectful and loving way.

Ladies, we have to be smart in choosing our men and our girlfriends. Your girlfriends should be those who are going to push you and inspire you to do better in your life. A real friend does not want to see you living a non-prosperous life, but they should want what is best for you whether you are single or married. Your boyfriend should be willing to accept you and your friends, and vice versa. Even if you know she is with a man who you know is treating her wrong and you try to talk to her, continue to be there for her because she is going to need you when the truth is finally revealed to her.

Girlfriend is such a good description of the roles they play in our lives. The word girl shows that they understand the emotions and experiences of a female. The word friend describes them as our ally, our comrade, our helper, and our pal. They are loyal, trustworthy, and willing to help when we need it. Girlfriends are placed in our lives so strategically so when one is weak the other is strong. They work together to ensure we experience happiness, fun, and a sense of belonging. Show love to your girlfriends today and thank them for their friendship. Thank them for the advice they gave even when you did not want to hear it. Thank them for being there during the difficult times, and most importantly thank God for sending them into your life. Nonetheless, as you continue your journey and Mr. Right continues searching for you, be hesitant to change your relationship status based on the status of your friends' relationships.

Reality Speaks: Choose your girlfriends wisely to ensure they will provide insightful wisdom.

Realistic Thinking

Based on the characteristics below, circle the characteristics that are most important to you when it comes to choosing your girlfriends. Feel free to add other attributes.

Loyal   Honest   Caring   Intelligent   Helpful   Fun

Dependable   Encouraging   Passionate   Risk Taker

Determined   Hard Worker   Amiable

Spiritual   Strong   Slow to Anger   Positive Attitude

Wise   Listener   Loving   Supportive   Kind   Genuine

Based on the same characteristics, circle the ones you feel your girlfriends possess.

Loyal   Honest   Caring   Intelligent   Helpful   Fun

Dependable   Encouraging   Passionate   Risk Taker

Determined   Hard Worker   Amiable

Spiritual   Strong   Slow to Anger   Positive Attitude

Wise   Listener   Loving   Supportive   Kind   Genuine

***Based on your findings, analyze your girlfriends' personalities to see if their personalities match or exceed your desired attributes.

The last time your girlfriends were honest with you about a situation and you knew they were telling the truth, how did you respond?

_____
_____
_____
_____
_____
_____
_____
_____

When it comes to my girlfriends, I have to remember ....

_____
_____
_____
_____
_____
_____
_____

Reality Checkpoint #6—Expectations and standards sound more like ultimatums.

A standard is known as a model, the criterion, or a benchmark. Our standards can be as simple as determining what we expect out of a restaurant, and become more specific and involved when determining our expectations for our first house purchase. When we eat at a restaurant we usually anticipate that the restaurant will provide quality customer service and exceptional food that will satisfy our hunger. If you were going to a fast food restaurant your standards would be slightly different than those you would have for an upscale restaurant and you would definitely expect to pay much more at the upscale restaurant. We create standards in order to have a measurement by which we can determine our level of satisfaction. If your standard for living is a nice home, family, and an average salary, then you know anything less will cause you to think you are living below your standards, and anything above it will exceed your standards. When it comes to men, why do we confuse our standards and make ultimatums instead? Moreover, why do we enter into new relationships without a clear understanding of our personal standards? Let us deal with the misunderstanding when we confuse the definition of standards with ultimatums.

One of the most common mistakes we make in our relationships with men is our misunderstanding of standards. We either: 1. Begin our relationships without knowledge of what our standards truly mean and confuse our standards with ultimatums, or 2. We lower our standards in order to cater to someone who is not even worth our time and effort. You may have heard, thought, or even said the following:

"I want a man who makes at least a million dollars. I want a man with no kids even though I have two. Are you my man or what because it has already been a month since we started dating? I have to have a light skinned man. I have to have a dark skinned man. You need to spend more time with me and less time with your family and friends. My man has to wear only the best of Polo and Kenneth Cole."

Each of those statements, and more, reflect on how we create standards that take the focus on our men, and places the focus on other things that do not relate to the type of person they truly are. When we turn our standards into ultimatums it causes us to miss the opportunity to meet the real man within. Ladies, do not get confused and think you cannot dream big and want the best in life, but understand that your standards should not contradict your character and values. Your standards should not force one to make a decision without any type of compromise or agreement that is not beneficial for both parties involved. For example, how can you ask for a man with no kids and you have kids yourself? How can you ask for a man who makes a certain amount of money, and you are living paycheck to paycheck? How can you ask for a man who has big dreams and wants to better himself when you are so reluctant to dream big or change anything about yourself? Even if you are making hundreds of thousands dollars or you do not have any kids, make sure you are not focused merely on the outside and material things. Today, there are so many women who only crave the dollar sign and material things. You have to ask yourself whether or not you are being fair and just or just being unrealistic. I understand if you prefer a man who does not have kids, but how can you really judge him when you have kids also? Let's say you meet a man who happens to have kids, but you do not have any. Just make sure you are being fair and just, and be smart in determining whether or not he is truly the one. Only you can decide if the situation is something worth fighting for. For example, if you demand he spend time with you instead of with his family and friends you are not giving him a chance to share his time with everyone. He is now backed up into a corner, which could ruin a number of relationships. Making someone choose their family and friends over you is not fair for both parties. Just think. The less time you spend around the family, the less they will have the opportunity to get to know you more.

Is there a misunderstanding?

When we enter the relationship and have a misunderstanding of what our standards are, we open the gate that leads to confusion between two people. For example, consider a relationship that starts off as a simple as a meet and greet and continues with phone calls back and forth for about a week, but immediately we assume we are in a relationship. W conclude that if we have been talking on the phone almost everyday then it has been long enough and he should want to make the relationship exclusive. Well, is that really a standard and realistic expectation to be with someone after getting to know him for such a short period of time? Women especially move too soon and expect too many things too soon. We expect for him to make us his girl or his woman. We expect to meet his parents and his friends after the first few phone calls. We expect for him to drop everything anytime during the day just to pay attention to us. Our "standards" soon become demands because we make unrealistic expectations to begin with. Why should he dedicate everything totally to you and he just met you in the club a week ago? Let's keep it real. Did you ever ask him if he is looking for a relationship or if he prefers to be single? I have met so many women who said he admitted how he was interested in just being friends, but they still found a way to put their feelings into it. They cried because they find out they're not the only woman in his life when clearly he admitted that he was not interested in being in a relationship. I have heard the women who go through this, and I have talked with the men who told their women the same thing. While she is spending time making sure she is faithful, he is sitting at home thinking he is still single because he never made the commitment. While she is referring to him as her boyfriend, he refers to her as, "that's just my friend. We just cool." The woman interprets the situation as a harsh break-up and places the guy in the doghouse; when all the while it turned out to be a simple misunderstanding.

The gray area

Why does this occur? Why do we get so involved and expect so much too soon when we really did not discuss anything in the beginning? In many situations I've observed, sex became a part of the relationship or the woman assumed too much too soon, which caused a conflict in the relationship. Where there is sex, there are emotions (for many women). We get emotionally involved and expect for him to get as involved as we do. I like to refer to this type of situation as the "gray" area. Think about white, black and a mixture of both. When you are in the white stage it is like a blank canvas with two people trying to get to know each other. Then you have the black stage where both parties have decided to be together and date exclusively. The gray area, for some, means you are dating, but not exclusively; or it means you two are just messing around. For others it simply means both partners are growing closer but they are hesitant to take their relationship to the next level in order to get to know each other more. Some even consider the gray area as the perfect spot to camp out because a real commitment is never made. It is the gray stage where miscommunication takes place and too much is unspoken. The woman assumes they are in a relationship while he still thinks of them as "just friends." Even though they are doing things as if they are in the relationship, either party has not established the relationship status. So what happens when you confront him on the issue? Most likely you will come off as needy or possessive because he thinks you are not comfortable with the idea of you two being just friends. Instead of waiting for months to bring up the issue, you should have discussed each other's expectations in the beginning.

I dated a gentleman for about eight months never knowing what our status was. It was obvious we were in the gray stage but I was confused as to what was really going on. I thought I was his girlfriend and we were exclusive because we did almost everything together. We would go on dates during the week. We would study together, cook and eat dinner together, travel together, and attend parties and dances together. I figured since we were doing things in the public eye and he was treating me like his girl, then I must have been his girl. Later, however, I found out he had a list of girls he was involved with. At the end of the eight months, I finally decided to approach him about becoming exclusive because I was under the impression that I was the only one. I wanted to have the title as his girlfriend, but of course he did not want that because he was totally fine with the stage that we were in. An old saying reminded me, "Why buy the cow when you can get the milk for free," and he was definitely reaping the benefits of being with me just as if he were my real boyfriend. There was no reason for us to take our relationship to the next level because he was satisfied with how things were. I was the only one who appeared to have a problem because I refused to share him with other females. Although some ladies are content with the concept of sharing their men, my standards at that time were to be exclusive with only one man and not allow someone to be with me and other women. I failed to discuss his and my expectations in the beginning, which meant I entered into a relationship without knowing exactly what he wanted and him knowing what I wanted. Of course I was heartbroken knowing that all of my effort, time, and strong like were wasted. Furthermore, I had to accept the responsibility for the situation because of my lack of communication and misunderstanding of his and my expectations. I could not just blame him for everything because in the end I was guilty of continuing something that I did not even know existed. It was like driving around and around to reach a certain destination, but refusing to stop and ask for directions to make sure I was going the right way.

Ladies, do not enter into something without knowing exactly what each person expects. Even if you are looking for a relationship it does not have to begin immediately. Take time to get to know him and even yourself before you presume that he wants the same things you want. If you take time in the beginning to be smart and wise with your decisions it could save you time and humiliation in the end.

If you have no direction, you'll keep driving in circles.

Sometimes even worse than confusing our standards and expectations, we make mistakes by lowering our standards to cater to our mate because we are so desperate, needy, or impatient. We are so desperate to find a man that we accept anything that has a cute smile and whispers sweet nothings in our ears. Our neediness causes us to feel as if we have to have a man regardless of who he is. We are so impatient that we do not want to wait for the right one to come along and instead we think every man we choose is "the one." Take a moment and think about your standards. What do you use as your criteria when considering how good a man is? Hopefully, your standards reflect loyalty, spirituality, trustworthiness, respect, compassion, and especially compatibility. It is difficult to be with someone if you are not compatible with that person, but it is even more difficult to be with someone who is reading a different book than you are. You are reading lover's lane while he is steadily reading the player's guide to pimping. You have to be open and honest about your standards and stay committed to your plan. If you begin the relationship declaring you will remain abstinent, then do not lower your standards by being with someone who craves sex. Do not lower your standards by staying with someone who treats you like you are worthless only because you think he is the finest man you have ever seen. If you want a man who is successful and strives to live an abundant life, then you know if you try to be with someone who has no drive or determination it will not last because you are reading two separate books.

You say you want to be with someone you can trust, but you choose to be with the guy who you know plays games and refuses to be faithful. You find a married man and you think he will leave his wife once he realizes how wonderful you are. Again, you are lowering your standards and accepting something less. Why should you be with someone else's husband when you deserve your own husband? You are worth more than that. You are basically saying that you do not care about honesty and loyalty, and you definitely do not have compassion for other women. You say you want a man who loves the Lord and is spiritual, but you lower your standards by being with a guy who rarely prays or even talks about his spirituality. Forcing him to go to church with you all of the time is definitely not the best approach to solving that problem. Then you are confused why you feel like something is missing or why you two cannot seem to connect beyond your physical attraction. You claim you want a man who will treat you with respect, but you refrain from making him work for your respect. How can he respect you if you do not respect yourself? You allow him to talk down to you or mistreat you without standing up for yourself. You declare you want a man who does not like to go out all of the time, but you search for your dream man every time you go out to the club. You say you want a man who loves you for you, while at the same time you are changing yourself in order to cater to what you think he likes. You become a sex driven woman, a money chasing female, or sports crazed fanatic when you know you hate sports in an attempt to show him how much you are willing to compromise. Compromise and changing the type of person you are is totally different. You can compromise with your partner without changing everything about yourself. Remember, compromise occurs when both parties are willing to cooperate, not when you sacrifice yourself to become what he wants you to be.

Be you even when he rejects you

After evaluating how much I was settling and lowering my standards, I realized how fake I had become. I was not being real with myself because I was changing everything about myself. It was not until I met my soul mate and realized I could totally be me and he would accept it, whether good or bad. He accepts who I am and more importantly I accept who I am. Instead of compromising my standards, we communicated early in the relationship, and compromise on those things that need it. In the past I would do anything to please my man but at the cost of losing my true measures of satisfaction—my personal standards. If he was reading books that did not promote growth or self-evaluation but talked about love and lust, then I was reading the same books. If he was content to going to church every now and then, somehow I became content with attending church every now and then. Again, he was becoming my everything as I was neglecting the source of my everything—God. When guys would disrespect me or say hurtful things, I would contemplate how I could change my actions and question my self worth or blame myself for all of the problems. If he wanted to watch ESPN all day instead of being productive, then I felt I had to watch ESPN all day to make sure we were spending time with each other. If he wanted to have sex when I knew in my heart it was the wrong thing to do, I was willing to let down my guard and justify why it was okay. This was by far the hardest for me to deal with at the end of the day. I was lowering my standards by settling for less than what I deserved. I wanted to stand firm and keep my standards, but I have to admit I was co-dependent and desperate to be with a man. When I realized how much I catered to so many different men by lowering my standards, I had to check myself. I was so quick to embrace their standards and how they wanted me to be, but neglected the standards that counted the most—God's standards. If I had been as dedicated to pleasing Him as I was when trying to please them, then a lot of things would have turned out completely different. We get caught up in the world's standards—weight, money, status, fashion, and relationships—and forget that it is only God's standards that really matter. Nevertheless, it happened and I learned from it all. I re-evaluated my standards and turned my impulsive decisions into patient and well thought out decisions. It is easy to get caught up in trying to please a man because we are so determined to find Mr. Right, but we have to be careful and make sure we have full awareness of who we are and whose standards we are living by.

Communicate—Speak into the microphone!

Have you ever thought back to a past relationship and could really noticed how different you were or realized that you put up with so much more than you should have? You put up with so much because you were fearful of letting go and keeping your standards. You may have thought the opposite and realized your standards were so unrealistic that you basically pushed the guy away. So how do we differentiate between what is enough and what is too much, and how can we compromise without compromising everything we believe?

One of the best things we can do is make sure we communicate openly with our partner. Your expectations for him may be completely different from his expectations for you, but you will never know until this is completely communicated to each other. As you two are dating, you may expect him to be with you and only you, but he may expect the two of you to date until your relationship is made exclusive. You may expect to spend every waking moment with him on the phone or in person, while he thinks hanging out every once in awhile is enough for him. As

I mentioned earlier, both of you have to be reading the same book and on the same page. Even when two people read a book they may interpret it in different ways. However, if you communicate effectively then you will eliminate any misunderstandings and you can make a sensible decision as to whether or not he meets, exceeds, or falls below your standards. Moreover, you will not have to waste time with someone for weeks, months, or even years knowing deep down inside they are nowhere on your level. If it seems as if every man you are with seems to perform below every one of your standards, then you may need to minimize the number of men you date to ensure the right man chooses you, or you may have to re-evaluate your standards.

In order to avoid lowering your expectations you have to think of yourself as deserving only the best. If you settle for anything less then you are admitting that you are willing to sacrifice yourself just to be with him. You are declaring a lack of self worth and refusing the virtue of patience. You can keep yourself and keep your man simultaneously if both of you know in the beginning what you are willing to sacrifice, and there is a clear understanding of expectations. However, when it seems like your expectations sound more like ultimatums, be prepared for him to refuse the challenge to avoid being forced into something he is not sure of or to eliminate feeling like he is being controlled by you.

Reality Speaks: Never assume what has yet to be acknowledged.

Realistic Thinking

Sounds Like (circle E or U)	Expectations	Ultimatum
"I want a man who makes at least 100,000/year so he can pay my bills."	E	U
"I want a man who isn't shy, and likes to be around people."	E	U
"I want a man who only drives a certain type of car."	E	U
"I only want a man who has at least a Master's Degree."	E	U
"I want a man who is trustworthy and loyal."	E	U
"I want a man who is similar in personality."	E	U
"I want a man with no kids so he only has to worry about taking care of my kids."	E	U
"I want a man who wants to spend all of his time with me."	E	U
"I want a man who enjoys doing different things like traveling, reading, or going to poetry lounges."	E	U
"I don't want a man with any kids."	E	U
"I want a man who is sensitive to my needs."	E	U
"I want a man who owns his own business."	E	U
"I want a man who will do whatever I tell him to do."	E	U
"I want a man who doesn't mind taking care of his woman and treating her like she deserves."	E	U

Share your answers and compare with others. Find out what others think about expectations and ultimatums.

Reality Checkpoint #7—"I think, therefore I am—Lonely!"

Obesity and being overweight has been the major topic for the last few years in our nation. We have tried numerous diet plans, attended weight loss meetings, tried different workout plans, and some have even stopped eating completely in an attempt to gain the "perfect body." Some lose the weight without struggle while others fight constantly trying to figure out why their weight continues to stay put. I, personally, have tried a number of workout plans and diets. I would research for information on the Internet and read magazines especially when the articles would advertise the new method to losing 50 pounds in a week. As I continued on this quest to find the "it" plan to lose weight I came across numerous articles and people who admitted the first thing that must occur is a change in your mindset. The mind is what separates the successful from the unsuccessful because it is all about your mindset and what you think you are capable of doing.

Think about yourself when you decided you wanted to shed some pounds but struggled to make it happen in the beginning. Most likely you lost hope or in your mind you did not think you could accomplish such a huge goal. There were times when I started a weight loss plan, but then I would get so discouraged because I did not see the results as fast as I wanted or my desire would not be great enough for me to lose weight. I would constantly play mind games with myself thinking I was not going capable of losing weight, or thinking that my eating lifestyle was not that bad. Eventually I realized how I had to make a lifestyle change and I began to stay consistent when I made up in my mind that I would not quit—no matter what. Beyond weight loss you may have struggled with an idea to start or own your own business. You see the dream being fulfilled but you allow your thoughts to deter you away from the idea. You think you lack the skill and intelligence when in actuality you dreamed this as a child so it must be something you are capable of doing. You are in constant struggle between what you want to do and what you think you CAN do. However, later in the chapter we will see that what we think we can do heavily impacts what we will do.

Through life, we have heard numerous statements that encourage self-motivation and self-help. We have been told to dream big and think big because how you perceive yourself will shape your life. Writers and speakers have emphasized how important it is to change our mindsets even when it comes to different aspects of our lives—careers, lifestyle, working out, and even in relationships. I have heard for years how you have to speak those things that are not as if they were. What does that mean? Why should I speak about something that does not even exist yet? How can I say I will live a prosperous life when clearly I am broke right now? Repeatedly, it has been said you are what you eat; moreover, I think we are what we think. If you think you are broke, then you will be broke. If you think you are dumb, you will act that way. If you think you are nothing more than a failure, then you will fail at everything. Furthermore, if you think you are lonely, guess what? You will be lonely.

Are you really alone?

Women have struggled with this battle of loneliness for some time now. We have been or may be in a situation where a man is missing in our lives, but we look around and our friends have a man and even your enemies have a man. Then, we assume the title of lonely, which can also be referred to as "without a friend in the world." Are you really without a friend in the world? Are you really alone and abandoned? You may be without a man, but what about the Man above? What about your friends and family who care about you and love you? Of course there are times when we feel like we are alone because we do not have a man there but maybe there is a reason why there is a man missing in the equation. Sometimes our lonely and depressive mindset will keep us in that state of mind. We speak the spirit of loneliness into our own lives because of bad decisions we make, and more importantly because we may be spending less time with the Father. For instance, my first chapter alludes to the issue of making your man your everything, and when he leaves you feel as if everything that completes your life has left you also. Our God is a jealous God, as He should be, because at the end of the day He is our everything. He is the friend we can call on when no one else is there and He speaks through His word to encourage, inspire, and help us through the good and bad situations of our lives. So, if your relationship is focused too much on your man, then maybe God is trying to turn your focus toward him so you will understand that you are NEVER alone.

If you do not have a man in your life, at the moment, do not claim loneliness over your life. Your loneliness can cause you to make impulsive and drastic decisions. Consider how you have lowered your standards, ignored your female intuition, changed yourself, engaged in sexual activity when you did not want to, and catered to his needs before catering to your emotional and physical needs. All of these things can occur out of pure desperation resulting in feelings of loneliness. When we think of desperation we think of some woman who is holding on to her man's coat tails crying and screaming begging for him to stay, which could be a reaction of desperation. Nevertheless, desperation is revealed in our actions, but in the end it was the mind that influenced our actions. Something in our minds caused us to have fear, extreme anxiety, or worry—all of which describe desperation. Our fear stems from fear of thinking we will never have a man. The extreme anxiety causes us to act without considering the consequences of our actions because we are so concerned with getting what we think we need or want as soon as possible. The worry is simply the worry of being alone for the rest of our lives, and sometimes we worry that we will not be able to live a prosperous life because we will not have a man to take care of us. These thoughts consume our minds and impact our interactions with men. You either know this type of woman because you have seen her or because you know the woman is you. You have seen her time and time again. She is in the club every weekend trying to find the man of her dreams. She comes to church praying only to find a man in the choir, in the pews, or even in the pulpit. She is the same woman who has a different boyfriend every month because she is constantly on the prowl for her husband. She surfs the Internet tirelessly hoping a single, fun, and charismatic lady will find the handsome, built, and talented gentleman. She attends the video shoot or waits patiently after the game in order to get the chance to be with a "baller" who will take care of her. She is begging and yearning for attention from men because she does not want to be alone for a minute, a year, or a lifetime. On the outside she plays the role of a "G" or a player, but her x-rays would reveal the diagnosis of woman suffering from lonesomeness. She claims to be with these different men because she thinks she is so good at being a player, when really different men are playing her emotionally and physically. She appears to be happy because she is playing the field, but if you catch her alone at home you will see a young and feeble heart who thinks she is not capable of living without a man. Simply put, she is lonely, but only because she chooses to accept this as a part of her life.

She may even be the woman who thinks all men are dogs, which results in her acting in the same manner. You cannot think all men are dogs and still attempt to find a man in a group you consider to be merely dogs. If you think all men are dogs and treat them in that manner, then he will act in that way. "All men are dogs" has been the claim to fame and the excuse women have used time and time again. We take pride in blaming the men for our loneliness. We blame the men who have left us for other women, who finally admitted they were gay, or the men who made the wrong decisions that landed them in prison. We find it easier to blame others because then we do not have to take responsibility for our actions, and it helps to justify the amount of time we spend wallowing in our self-pity. I have even known women who use the line repeatedly "men are dogs," but they are guilty of the same wrongdoings. They have cheated with married women, or other women's boyfriends. They have manipulated men into becoming their sugar daddy without considering the fact that he needs money to supply for his own family. Nonetheless, they still remain lonely because the men do not provide the cure to their loneliness.

Who's to blame for our lonely and abandoned way of thinking?

So, I ask, who is the man really the only one to blame for our loneliness? Yes, there are times when we meet guys who treat us wrong and do things that cause us to be alone, but blaming the other party does not always support our reasons for being alone. I experienced the stages of bitterness when I thought every man was a dog and every man only wanted one thing from me. I used to say all of the time how I was never going to find the right man. I even tried to play the vengeful character by trying to treat men like they had treated me, until I did a self-evaluation. I realized that no matter how many men I had been with I was the common denominator in all of the relationships. I had to take ownership of my actions and my mistakes just as I was trying to make the men take responsibility of their actions. Although there were times I was alone, it was my decision to be lonely and act as if I did not have anyone in my life. I was the one who thought I had to have a man in my life to complete me, not him. It was I, not him, who thought men were the source of my happiness. I was the one who made everything in my life revolve around guys who caused me to feel like I was missing something because when he left, I thought my joy left.

I remember a time when I really let my mind take over my actions because I became so consumed with my ex. We dated for a while but then reached the periods of breaking up and getting back together. You know how it is when you are with someone and you pretty much know the relationship is over but you do everything in your power to try and hold on. This is exactly what was going on. The last phase of our relationship he broke up with me and I acted somewhat shocked even though I knew deep down inside he had been acting differently and treating me differently. I could tell he was unhappy and honestly I was unhappy too. So, instead of accepting his recommendation for us to separate I acted as if we needed to hold onto the "love" and try and work things out. I'll admit it I actually cried and pleaded for him to give us another chance. I gave reason after reason as to why we should stay together. Now, I just mentioned how I knew how unhappy we both were, and I knew he wanted to be with someone else, but my desperate heart would not allow him to leave me. Although I did not go to the extremes of stalking him and holding onto his coat tails, I was holding onto him with my heart and mind. I was on the phone pleading with him trying to make him stay with me. I could not accept us being apart because in doing this I had to accept being alone without a man and I was not ready for that (so I thought). I had put so much energy and time into him that I forgot to take care of myself. When the conversation finally ended I immediately called my mother and admitted that I needed to come home for a little. My state of mind was so confused that I found myself depressed. I allowed sadness and despair to take over my body. There was a commercial that explained how depression hurts every-where and it is so true. Depression was hurting my heart because all I wanted to do was cry all of the time. My body was affected because all I wanted to do was sleep the pain away. Even my friends and family were affected because I could not be the fun, optimistic, and electrify-ing friend they knew. Some may even be thinking now I would never let myself go just because of some man, and I sincerely pray that you do not, but to those women who have been there you know exactly what I am talking about. You can come out of the situation victorious. You can overcome the depression, sadness, and bitterness because God gives us the strength and power to do just that. Moreover, there are so many things to consider than just the small affairs of a failed relationship. After a week passed, I gained my composure back and prayed to God that I would never let a man bring me to that point in my life ever again. I prayed for Him to take control over my life and I asked for the subservi-ent spirit so I could allow Him to do what was best for me. It is easy to ask God to take control over our situations, but we have to be willing to submit to His will no matter what our personal agenda may be.

After the incident I knew it was time for me to be alone and learn how to be single. You can be alone and single and refuse to feel as if you have no one in your life. When I say learn how to be single I am referring to being single and happy. I am talking about being single and having an appreciative and satisfied attitude whether we are dating are just spending time alone. Reality check: we have to learn to love us before creating an "us" between ourselves and another man. Sometimes when we are single, we assume it gives us a reason to be unhappy and dismal. Our attitude reflects the attitude of a woman who is unhappy. Instead of claiming that I was lonely I proclaimed God as my everything and all that I needed. Anything that God provided in addition to his love and support exceeded my needs and wants. During the times when I was single, I had to learn where to direct my focus and attention. If our minds are constantly worrying about being lonely and finding a man then we will make mistakes by entering in relationships that do not add value to our lives. We date the married men, covet our friends' men, ruin other people's relationships, and even ruin our own relationships.

Overall, I knew I had to find the true source of my joy and rely on Him as my everything. We have to take ownership of our mistakes also and recognize that being alone does not have to mean we are pathetic, and it does not have to mean it will last for eternity. Just because you are single does not mean you have to claim loneliness over the rest of your life and look at the situation through the lens of pessimistic eyes. Our temporary stage of being alone, no matter how long it lasts, should be used to our advantage. You may say how is this temporary when I have been single for years? Temporary simply means it does not last forever, so if you are still alive and breathing, then it still may be in His will for you to meet someone. Think about your current financial situation in the same way. Even though you think you are currently broke, do you plan on being broke for the rest of your life? Being broke is a state of mind. Instead, refer to your situation as: "your funds are temporarily depleted." You have to say the same thing about your relationships with men and make sure that the search for your husband is aligned with God plans for your life. Do not simply pray, "Lord, please send me a good man and a husband." You have to pray, "Lord if it is in your will let thy will be done. If and when you send a man my way, I pray that I am spiritually ready for what you have for me." Understand that you are not on a search for a goldmine. He is searching for you because the Bible clearly states, "a man who findeth a wife, finds a good thing." During your "waiting period" you have to find meaningful things to do and understand that your time should be used effectively.

The Waiting Room

Prevent yourself from focusing on how lonely you are during the waiting period, and use the time to improve yourself. Did you ever wonder why God allowed the relationship to end or caused the door to close to a potential relationship? Sometimes He is trying to transfer our attention from the insignificant circumstances of our lives to the most important. Other times he is trying to release that man from our lives because he has so much more in store for us. As a single woman, this is the perfect opportunity to serve others and grow as a woman. It is the waiting period that allows you to study His word, grow in His spirit, and worship him more. When you have a man and eventually get married, your husband and family become very important and they will consume much of your time. When you are single, you do not have the same everyday tasks that a married woman would have. Moreover, the idle time you have can be used to serve in a ministry such as singing in the choir, ushering, providing hospitality, working with the assimilation ministry, and even embarking on a mission trip. It is so important to learn more about Him and grow with Him because then you will gain a better understanding of His will in your life. Whenever you want to get to know someone you have to spend more time with the person, and the same is true with God. If you really want to do his will, hear Him when He speaks, and do not confuse Him with other voices you may hear, then you have to spend more time with the Father. When you do this you will experience his love and compassion and you will grasp a better understanding of what it is He wants in your life.

I have had plenty of waiting periods in my life. At first I did things that hindered my growth as a woman. I would party all of the time thinking I would eventually meet my man. I would call different guys and spend time with them trying to eliminate the feeling of loneliness. I perpetrated to my girls and my friends acting as if I was okay with being single. The famous cliché of "single and ready to mingle" was my mentality. I thought enjoying singleness meant dating all kinds of guys all of the time. Although you can date when you are single, there comes a time for many, when you may just need to be single and be by yourself completely. It was not until later when I realized singleness, for me, was a time for me to gain a better understanding of what I needed for my life. During my useful waiting periods I took time to study His word more, I focused on things I wanted to accomplish in my own life. I began to see a vision for my life, and the plan as to how I could get there. No longer was I overly consumed in what I thought my man needed; rather I was focused on bettering my life and preparing for my husband so when in fact my husband showed up I knew I would be prepared for him.

During your waiting period, you have to make sure you spend time with yourself to ensure you have a better understanding of who you really are. The worst thing you can do is enter into a relationship without loving and knowing yourself because if you do, you will become something you are not, and you will allow someone else to determine your self-worth. A man cannot make you love and feel good about yourself. You have to learn how to self-love even when no one else seems to love you. Sometimes you have to learn how to be alone and be content with your situation no matter what the situation may be. You cannot fully rely on the man to be there whenever you want to do something that you think requires a man's presence. If you want to go to the movies, eat at your favorite restaurant, take up bowling or whatever your interests, do it, girl! Your life does not stop or go because of a man. I know, sometimes you want to have a guy around to talk to and to do things with, but you should not choose any type of man to share your life with. This should be done with sincere thought and prayer. Realize that your waiting period is merely the time between now and what is to come. Your latter will be greater and you do not have to reside in your loneliness, but you can reside in the spirit of hope and joy. Think of your waiting period as the provisional parking space preparing you for your potential partner.

Reality Speaks: "It's been said "the mind is a terrible thing to waste"; so, quit wasting time thinking about how lonely you are!

Realistic Thinking

Besides your partner, list *at least* 10 other people in your life you talk to on a regular basis (weekly, monthly, or even annually). Keep these in mind or contact them when you begin to feel lonely. If you cannot think of ten, find a way to add more to your list.

1. _____   6. _____
2. _____   7. _____
3. _____   8. _____
4. _____   9. _____
5. _____   10. _____

When you begin to feel lonely, what are some things you can do to eliminate the feeling from taking over your mind and your thoughts?

_____
_____
_____
_____
_____
_____
_____
_____
_____
_____

From now on, when I begin to feel overly sad and depressed because I'm alone, I will ....

_____
_____
_____
_____
_____
_____
_____
_____
_____
_____

Reality Checkpoint # 8—Looking for money, mansions, and mo' money, instead of a man.

One of our favorite things to do as women is to go shopping. Shopping is an experience we love to have when we want the latest fashions, the cute little black dress, the accessories that will match our outfit, and of course the shoes that are drop dead gorgeous. We enter the mall with a mission determined to find the perfect outfit. My closest friends know that when I go shopping I could potentially spend approximately 2–3 hours in the mall per experience. It is rare that I will go to the mall, if I'm shopping for myself, and spend less than an hour in the mall. My method to the madness is to skim and go through the entire mall and look at the different designs. I am not an impulsive shopper so I like to know I am getting the best deal for my money. If I see a dress in one store for fifty dollars, but I see a similar dress in another store for a lower price then I will most likely buy the lesser of the two. Even though my friends may not spend quite as much time as I spend in the mall, they still utilize a lot of time because they try on different outfits, shoes, or dresses to make sure they choose the one that will look the best. The worst thing is to go to the mall, purchase a shirt, and later realize we do not like the shirt at all. It hangs in our closet for years, or we just decide to give it away to someone because we never really liked it to begin with.

So, if we spend so much time selecting the "perfect" outfit, the hottest pair of shoes, or the cutest dress, why do we choose our men with less contemplation? Usually when we enter the mall we know exactly what we want and if we do not find it, then we will not simply buy anything. Instead, we may leave and go to another store or mall in hopes of finding what we truly want. This mentality can be viewed from two different angles when we are considering the gentlemen we want to date. We do one of two things: a. we decide in our minds we want a man who is "balling" (making a lot of money or has a lot of money) and will accept nothing less, or b. we do not spend enough time figuring out exactly what it is we want. Which one are you most likely guilty of doing? Are you the type who looks for the man who is balling out of control with money and refuses to look at the inner self? Or are you the type who doesn't even know the type of man she wants and just shops around until she finds the right guy? Honestly, I've taken on both of these roles during the course of my life, and I wasted plenty of time by taking on these two different perspectives. Although these types have been readily accepted in our society because everyone has the "got to get mine" mentality, it does not mean it is always healthy for us—especially those who are very emotional.

Digging for Gold

You know her, have seen her, or you may even be her. Let's deal with the gold digger. For some who may be confused with the term of "gold digger," a gold digger is simply a woman who chases after men merely for their cash and bank accounts. When I looked at words similar to digger (or dig), and I found words like excavate, hollow out, and even the verb hoe (referring to part of a gardening processing). They are trying to dig out and excavate as much money as they possibly can from the men. Gold diggers have been around for a while and we usually associate them with those ladies who hang around after the NBA/NFL games waiting for a chance to get close to the stars. We think of the groupies who follow around stars hoping for a chance to be their next project. We even consider some of the video vixens that decide to participate in the gold digging schemes just to get ahead and become the main star. We even consider the women we encounter on an everyday basis who chase the top executives in hopes of gaining the promotion.

There are so many different types of gold diggers and too many categories to analyze, but I want to take a moment and consider the issue of gold digging. Gold digging will bring us exactly what we want which is money, but what happens when you want more than that and deep down inside you know you are looking for Mr. Right? What happens when the money is cut off and you have been through the different musicians, artists, actors, executives, or even drug dealers but are still left alone with not a penny in your hand? Furthermore, what will happen when someone's emotions become involved? I know. You think you are hustling and just making sure you are set for the rest of your life by having a man take care of your financial needs, but the Bible teaches us that the love of money is the root of all evil. Your mind and heart is consumed with thoughts of money and dollar signs. You think money will solve all of your problems including your emotional and spiritual problems. You are no longer thinking of anyone else except yourself and are taking on an evil role because now your main goal is to find a rich or wealthy man and you will stop at nothing to get what you want. When the time comes and you meet the type of man you really want to be with, he will be overshadowed by your love and useless passion for money.

For the love of money

Why do you gold dig? Gold diggers often receive a lot of criticism and we never look at the reasons why. I understand you have struggled all of your life and you want better for yourself. You may have even avoided struggle all of your life and are looking for someone to continue the tradition, but none of the reasons are good reasons for chasing the money. Some women are diligently pursuing men who have money in hopes of making it big into the upper class. The money becomes the basis for the relationship that later turns into a marriage, and eventually results in divorce because the wrong type of love was present—love for money. You say you want a man who will treat you right and love you for you, but how can you say that when you are actively pursuing the wrong things.

Consider the following situations. Would you rather have a man with a lot of money who neglects to spend time with you? Would you prefer to have a rich man who makes you do everything for him no matter what the request may be? Would you choose to have a man who travels all of the time and never makes time for you, but provides financial stability for you every month? Would you rather have a man who never wants to marry you despite the number of years you all have been together, but still provides you with a weekly check for you to go shopping? Would you rather have a man who hits on you and calls you names, but continues to shower you with love through his money? Would you be willing to have nothing more than a sexual relationship just to receive a check at the end of the month to pay your bills and go shopping? Would you rather eliminate having an exclusive relationship in exchange for all of the latest fashions and shoes? Would you risk your family's life by being with the main drug dealer in the city so you will reap the benefits of his profits? Would you rather have a man who is married or in a relationship with another woman, but pays your house and car note on a monthly basis? Would you rather have a man who only associates with you in private because he refuses to be with you in public, but provides all of your monthly necessities and wants? If you have answered yes to any of these questions, you might be a gold digger. Why? You are willing to degrade your body and your character just to receive money. You are making an exchange for lies, deceit, sex, and happiness just so you will look the best in your new outfits, smell good with your new perfume, and walk with confidence with your new pair of stilettos. Do you not think you are worth more than 1000, 100,000, or even 1 million dollars? Sweetheart, you are priceless. There is no amount in the world that could afford you. As a woman you are the one who can bring forth life, nurture, and mature it. Your body was designed for life and when you decide to depreciate the value of your self-worth, you begin living beneath your full potential. Take inventory of your product and know that you are worth more than any dollar amount imaginable. You were already bought with a price and no one can even come close to making the same type of sacrifice.

Let us consider for a moment the gold digger who overlooks the girlfriend, the wife, or even the family. She makes no mention to the other parties involved simply to avoid having to deal with the guilt and shame living within her. She persistently chases after the top executive even though she notices the pictures of his family on his desk. She pursues the NBA/NFL star even though she sees the family faithfully attending the home games and cheering him on in the crowd. Although they have a secret relationship on the set of the video, she is still aware of the wife and kids who are waiting at home for him to return. What inside of her makes her continue in her evil ways and secret lies? Believe the Gospel when it says that the LOVE of money is the root of all evil. Think about it. If her mind was more focused on finding a man who would treat her like a woman should be treated, she would not only respect herself but she would also respect other women. Now, because she wants nothing less than the 1,000,000-dollar man, she will stop at nothing just to have him. I have seen gold diggers tear up marriages and families simply because of their selfish motives. What if you were the other woman? How would you feel or react? Women are sometimes envious of others and covet those things that do not belong to them, not realizing how their selfish ways are causing destruction in another person's life. Even those who chase after the man who is single but extremely wealthy take on the same type of attitude of going after what they think belongs to them. She no longer sees him as a man or potential mate, but she sees him as a dollar sign waiting to be used by her.

When opportunity knocks, answer the door!

When we chase after the money and those things that matter least in a healthy relationship, we miss out on the opportunity to experience true love. If you are wondering why you have yet to meet Mr. Right, think about your mentality. Is your mind consumed with money, mansions, and material things? Do you pray for mansions, fashion, and platinum jewelry instead of praying and asking for the right kind of man to enter into your life? Many of us have been guilty of this before. You remember the guy in school or college that was so into you, but you ignored him time and time again because he did not have as much money as you wanted. Maybe you were in the relationship with David, but David was struggling a little with his funds. Instead of staying with him through thick and thin, you decided you had to let him go because he was not taking you out to eat enough or buying you things all of the time. Later, you found out David was doing well and was promoted on the job, or decided to start his own business. I bet you would have given David a chance then had things been different.

We have seen it on television and in movies. The guy starts off with little money, but deep down inside he has this drive, dream, and determination to achieve so much. When he needs your support and encouragement through the rough times, you neglect him and determine he cannot provide for you right now. Your mind is merely focused on the right now, and not what he is capable of doing in the future. Do not confuse this type of situation with those who allow their men to just sit around for years and years not doing anything, and make the woman take care of everything. I am referring to the man whose funds may be temporarily insufficient because he is trying to make it through school or his job just laid him off and he is currently in the process of changing his career. The amount of money he makes cannot be the only thing you think about when determining whether or not he is the man for you. Most men appreciate a woman who will not give up on him during the struggling times, and will reward her later for her dedication. When he meets this type of woman, he does not have to worry about hidden motives and whether or not she is with him for the money. Even in the traditional wedding vows it states "for richer or poorer" because the writer realized that love is not based on how rich or poor you may be. It does play a role because you definitely do not want to be with someone who is not a good steward over money. However, you have to strategically choose the type of man you want to be with, and money should not be the desire that pushes you toward your "dream man." Many women, and men, make the mistake of marrying for money and forget that it love holds the bond together. The money will come and go, but if you steadily maintain the love and compassion within, then you can make it through the good and bad times.

You don't know her story

A lot of times with money you will find fame, titles, positions, and new levels of acknowledgement. You think you will no longer be considered the bad girl from the hood or the girl next door because now you will have a new title. Women look in the pulpit and see the Pastor or the ministers and conclude that they can see themselves as a preacher's wife. People seek to fit in and want to feel like they belong somewhere. They want to be known and they want to be famous without even knowing what it took for someone else to reach the same status. When we look on television we see the wives and the girlfriends of the stars and we think that is the life we want to live.

"Ooooh. What I wouldn't give to be her. I wish I were his girl. I bet she has it all. I want the same thing." When you hear these types of statements, you are hearing someone who wants to be like someone else at any cost just to say she has a lot of money or a man who has a lot of money. Instead of being a good wife or girlfriend you would rather be referred to as one or more of the following: a superstar's girl, his trophy wife, his gold digging boo, his sidekick, his secret love on the side, or his number one boo (out of 10 others). It is appropriate to want more for your life, but you have to want things for the right reasons. You see women fighting over different men because they want the limelight and they want the position as the head woman in his life.

You have to think, however, do you really know what the women on television, in the videos, or in the movies really have to go through, and would you really be willing to endure the things they have experienced? When he is constantly on the road or girls are constantly calling your phone or even cheating with your man, are those the types of things you want to deal with just to say you are his woman? It is so easy to get caught up in the dreams of others, but what is your own dream? How do you plan on making your OWN money instead of taking his? You should want more for yourself by doing more for yourself. No one can do for you what you cannot do for yourself. You should not wait for your "dream man" to come along on his white horse with a million dollars in his pocket. If he does come along and he is in fact wealthy, then accept him for who he really is and not simply because of his money. Get to know the true man inside to prevent yourself from making a terrible mistake. Find out how he feels about women, family, having children and not just how much is in his bank account.

There was a time when I was caught up in the money, fame, and titles. Thankfully the period did not last long, but it was long enough to waste enough time that could have been used in another way. I went through the phase of wanting to date the basketball star and trying to be with musicians. I grew up in a small town so dating a musician or one of the college basketball star athletes was considered "royalty." The musician I dated was someone I did not spend any time getting to know prior to becoming involved with him. I was so caught up in the fact that he was a musician who traveled all of the time that I thought eventually I would be able to live the same type of lifestyle. My passion for music also played a role, but the fact that he was in a position that elevated him in the church was the source of my desire. It may seem difficult to understand but it is a true situation for so many women. He was known by so many across the community, city, and even the nation because he played for so many different artists. I wanted to experience the same recognition by becoming his girlfriend. During the relationship, I thought I was the new girl in his life even though I knew he and his ex-girlfriend were just coming out of a long relationship. I thought I would take his mind off of her and make him see that we would look good together when we had to attend concerts and travel out of town. Eventually, reality checked in and he decided to end the relationship. He decided he wanted to be with his ex-girlfriend instead. So, all of the work I put into trying to make the relationship work was in vain because my heart and mind did not correlate with my actions. My actions appeared to be genuine, loving, and compassionate, but my mind was totally focused on being "his girl" instead of just being a good woman.

On another occasion, I decided I would try the infamous star athletes. In college, I dated (if you want to call it that) one of the basketball athletes. This time, I decided I wanted to experience the life as the girlfriend of a star athlete. Honestly, I thought he would eventually sign a multi-million dollar contract and I wanted to be included as part of the deal. I knew I would benefit tremendously if I were his girl. I knew all of the drama and chaos other girlfriends experienced, but I was willing to take the chance to see if I had what it took to be his girl. Unlike my relationship with the musician, I actually knew exactly how this athlete was because it was obvious in his actions. During our "relationship," we rarely talked and if we did we usually argued. He never respected me and I really did not make him because I was trying to get my hustle going—so I thought. I was not concerned about gaining his respect; rather I was more concerned with how I was going to maintain my status as his number one female. I knew he was messing around with other people, and I really did not care. Nevertheless, I did not care about myself because I was willing to hustle for something that was not meant for me, and I sacrificed who I was in the midst of it all. He would literally call me, we would argue, and next thing you know we were together at his place. There were no true feelings between either of us and ultimately everything ended because it was going absolutely nowhere. What was the purpose of all of it? The purpose was for me to see that money and status means absolutely nothing. When you sacrifice what matters the most in exchange for money you are left with nothing, even your pride and dignity. I ended the so-called relationship after doing a self-inventory and acknowledging that I could be successful with or without a man with a huge bank account.

Looking for the money, mansions, and mo' money could in fact provide you with every material item you want. What good is it, however, to have a large home with no one to share it with? What good is it to have a designer purse with thousands of dollars in it, but no one to share your money with? Do not end up like the woman who is lost and without anything because she relied on her sugar daddy to provide everything including the house, the dog, the car, and all of the money. When he leaves, the money leaves too. Then what will you do? You should look beyond how much is in his bank account and look to see how much is in his heart. The same effort you used to find the man with all of the money is the same effort you should use to find the man who has all of the loyalty, commitment, compassion, and love for you. If you continue gold digging and looking for a man for all the wrong reasons, you in return will be loved and used for all the wrong reasons.

Reality Speaks: Quit searching for your "get rich quick" man, and allow the "got it together" man to find you!

Realistic Thinking

When it comes to a mate, write down 10 MUST HAVE QUALITIES you feel are important for your partner to have in order to be compatible with you. Put a star next to the top three.

1.   6.
2.   7.
3.   8.
4.   9.
5.   10.

Out of ALL of the men you've dated, how many possessed most of the qualities listed above?

_____

_____

_____

For each set, circle the one that is more important to you. Discuss your findings with others and analyze your choices.	
A Man with money	**A Man with less money ....**
Who has no respect for women	Who respects women who deserve it
Who never spends time with his woman	Who tries to share his time with those he cares about
Who takes you on shopping spree every week	Who saves his money so he can eventually buy you two a house when you get married
Who gives money to you and other women	Who is currently in school trying to make more money
Who lies and cheats every now and then	Who is honest all of the time
Who shares his money with you, his wife, and his family	Who is single and ready to meet his soul mate
Who is conceited and boastful	Who is humble and appreciative of everything he has
Who never commits to one person	Who only commits to one person
Who cares only about his money and what he can do with it	Who cares about having enough money, but also cares about others

Reality Checkpoint #9—Trying to turn boys into men.

As an infant, we come out of the womb and no one expects us to immediately start walking because our limbs and bones have not fully developed. When we attend elementary school, our teachers educate us about things we should be familiar with based on our ages and brain capabilities. In middle school we finally begin the strenuous stages of mathematics and science, and learn how to use formulas to solve equations. For most, algebra becomes the benchmark for middle school students to know and understand before moving further. In high school, the pace increases and the work becomes a little more difficult. Even though we move toward our teenage years, we are still monitored closely because the administration admits that even teenagers may not be fully mature and ready to accept responsibility for their actions. They prepare us for post-secondary options such as college, technical school, or even the corporate sector. During college or the post-secondary season of our lives, we soon learn how to become more independent through life's lessons. We learn how to interact and work collectively as a team with others whether we want to or not, and most of all we learn a lot about ourselves. Even learning about ourselves takes time and effort because we have to be willing to accept our strengths and weaknesses no matter how others may perceive us.

As we experience the different stages of life, we fail, we succeed, we grow, we change, and we gain a better understanding of who we truly are. So, if we all experience these different stages of life, why do we assume everyone is at the same stage at the time? Furthermore, why do we assume some guys as the role of men when in fact they are still boys? Men grow at different stages just as women and children do. We always blame the guy for acting young or being mature and sometimes this is true. However, you have to know how to distinguish between a man and a boy. You cannot assume primarily because of his age that he is automatically considered a grown man. To say that one is a man means they take on the responsibilities of a man and do not simply use the title to explain who they are. Sometimes we make the mistake of auditioning everyone to play one of the major roles in our lives—the man, our partner, or our husband—only to find out later that he was not even close to the man we wanted. Then, we finally end up with a real man and cannot accept his manly ways because we are so used to dating boys.

When I met my soul mate, the first real man I ever dated, he treated me, and still does, like a woman should be treated. He respects my opinions, treats me with the utmost respect, and conducts himself like a gentleman all of the time. From opening doors, to taking care of me when I am sick, he treats me like I have never been treated before. I did not know how to accept his genuine love and kindness. In the beginning of our relationship, I used to tease him all of the time telling him the love and gentleman ways would only last for a few weeks and even months. To my surprise his loving ways never ceased. I always prayed for God to send me someone who would treat me like I deserved and He blessed me beyond what I imagined. At the same time I was paranoid thinking that his kind spirit would merely last for a season. I remember saying to myself, "Wow. This is what it feels like to really date a man." Most of the men I experienced before him were considered young men who were not fully developed into the man they claimed to be, and honestly I was not fully developed into the woman I was called to be.

Boys will be boys

Reflect for a moment on the guys you have dated up until now. Think about their actions and the numerous times you dealt with his immature ways and avoided moving on to something new and better. Despite his immature and childish ways, you were the one who continued in the relationship. Maybe he was not immature and childish, but his actions reflected his resistance toward becoming a true man. We have all dealt with the variety of men who fit into the category of what many refer to as "not being ready." For instance, consider your high school and even college mates. He roams the halls and campus showing off and flattering ladies with his charm, and approaches you to persuade you to enter into a relationship with him. At first he starts off as if he can deal with being an exclusive one-woman man, but soon realizes he is not quite ready. You, on the other hand, get upset and try to force him to get ready. You question why he does not want to be with you and why he felt the need to convince you to be with him when he knew he was not ready. Reality check: The truth of the matter is that you knew he was not ready. You noticed his actions and how he interacted with others, and you knew he was not ready for a relationship. Nevertheless, you pursued the relationship and now you are confused as to why he is not fulfilling the role you thought he was designed for. There were situations when I knew he was too young in the mind and we were not on the same page. I was more interested in being in a relationship, while they were still trying to play the field by dating different females. I would play mind games with myself by saying, "I know he wants to be with me. He just needs time. Why is he running away from the man he really is?" He was not running away from anything. This just happened to be the stage in his life he had yet experienced. How could I expect him to be a man when he was still yet a boy, and I, myself, was still a young lady?

There are those men who we try to change who enjoy placing their hands on a lady's body through excessive abuse. We experience his abuse both physically, mentally, and verbally but somehow we make excuses for his behavior and think he will change his actions and become a man. We have seen them on different television shows and we have heard their stories as it relates to their husbands or boyfriends who continuously abuse them, and sometimes even their kids. When asked why they stay the simple reply is usually because they love him. Many times we put up with the abuse because we do not first love ourselves, which causes us to accept any kind of treatment from others. Furthermore, there is this feeling deep within us that cause us to believe that he will actually change his habits. Time and time again he apologizes and says he will get help, but the process never begins and the abuse continues. He's not ready to start over and become the real man he should be. For some reason, he is comfortable with his current state and refuses to change for anyone else. He cannot see the hurt and pain he is causing others who he claims to have real love for. If you are in an abusive relationship you have to know that you cannot change him. You may not be able to change him, but know that you can change the situation. You will never find your Prince Charming if you spend the rest of your life with someone who doesn't love you anyway. Love does not beat, hit, shove, push, verbally abuse, or even mentally abuse. Real love comforts, shows compassion, and makes you feel secure. It shouldn't make you feel weak, useless, and torn apart. You have to want better for yourself and you must put your plan into action in order to get what you deserve.

Know when you are too old for games

There are other guys we try to turn into men and they are known as the guys who are used to playing games with women because no one has truly made them step up to the plate. You are with him and wonder why he continuously seems to play games all of the time. He acts like an annoying or immature child who loves to play games just to get what he wants. He says he will call you back and you wait for him by the phone and he never returns your call. He says he will make more time for you, but fails to make any plans for you during his busy schedule. He merely calls when he needs something and expects you to be there at his beckon call. Promise after promise is broken and you are left wondering if he is really serious about you and your relationship. He basically thinks you will do everything for him because that is what he is used to. He thinks of you as a loving mother who spoils her children and thinks you in turn will spoil him and let him get away with anything. How will he change into a grown man who does not have to play games and actually takes his relationship seriously when you are encouraging his behavior by falling into the trap? You say you are strong and you will not let any man treat you wrong, but you are still waiting by the phone tirelessly just in case he calls and needs you. Whenever he claims he needs you, you drop everything to cater to him and what he wants. You neglect your friends and family quickly just to ensure all of his so-called needs are met. You play right into his tricks and the games he is used to playing. Now, he expects for all women to cater to him like he is KING. Do not get me wrong. When you find a good man, you should treat him good as long as he is doing the same for you. Otherwise, you will put all of your energy and time into someone who refuses to do the same, and you wear yourself out for the real one who will actually come and sweep you off your feet. Some guys simply play games because they know they can get away with it and they still have a childish mindset, but a man will do whatever his woman will deal with. You cannot change him into a real man who wants to eliminate games from his relationship without making sure you are not contributing to his behavior. If you allow him to keep playing games then you will always be defeated in the game of love.

Some women even like a man who appears to be a challenge for them because they feel accomplished as if they have conquered something. He never gives them attention, he rarely calls, or he even gives you and everyone else attention. He is still a boy, not yet a man ready to own up to his responsibility as a man who is serious about going to the next level in his relationship. So, women, how long will you allow the challenge to last? Is this challenge worth you experiencing pain and confusion for months, years, or even the rest of your life? You may be so caught up in him and the grand challenge that you miss out on the real challenge that will come—being in love.

Young Puppy Love

I dated a guy for a while and for a brief moment I thought we were really going to take our relationship to the next level. Although he was younger than me, I really thought we were on the same level. I just knew he wanted to be in a relationship even though he really had not experienced a real relationship for quite some time. At first the relationship started off great and we were really having a fun time. Later, the calls lessened and the time spent together was almost non-existent. I was confused wondering what was really going on. I could not understand why something I thought was so great was now turning into nothing. I was waiting by the phone waiting for him to call. If he said we were going to go out on the weekends I was waiting and willing to drop everything. I was under the impression he was busy with studying and was using his time to ensure he performed to the best of his ability so he would graduate successfully. Deep down inside I had this feeling that something else was going on and things just did not seem right.

I could see the change happening in him, but I still thought he would realize what we had and would change his ways again. I noticed how he was more concerned with partying and spending more time with his friends instead of me. I even questioned him about wanting to be single so he would not have to stay with me and be unhappy, but he would try to convince me otherwise. I knew we were on two different levels because he was still interested in doing things a young man wanted which was conflicting with what a woman wanted. Unfortunately after months passed I learned that all of my fears and thoughts were true. He had lied to me repeatedly about his whereabouts and activities he was involved in. He made me think everything about our relationship was fine, when in actuality he was interested in other ladies. At first I was confused, hurt, and still trying to work things out because I could not understand why he would ruin our relationship. Nonetheless, I later realized that he were simply on two different pages. I was ready for a serious relationship, while he was still ready to play games and mess around with different women. In the back of my mind I always knew it was going to happen because there were some things he had yet experienced, but I had already been there and done that. I knew it was only a matter of time before he would want the freedom and choice to do whatever he wanted to do, but I thought our relationship would change his views. I was not willing to allow him to be with me and do whatever he wanted, so the relationship ended of course. Moreover, if I had been less concerned with changing his actions and more concerned with giving him time to grow into his manhood, then maybe I would have eliminated the amount of hurt and pain I endured during that time.

Change and growth is inevitable.

When we think we can simply change a young man or boy into a man, we are trying to force something to happen that we do not have the control to do. Similarly to chapter four, we try to change something we do not have control over. The last thing a man wants to feel is that another woman is controlling him. We have to let them experience the different levels of growth and manhood on their own time because everyone grows and changes at different times. Furthermore, if you know you are in a relationship with someone you feel is too young for you, then you need to make the most important change and say goodbye to the relationship until he is ready to be the man you need in your life. The separation may last for a while, and it may last forever, but if you do not allow it to happen then the time will be made up somehow whether now or later. I have seen so many enter into relationships with guys who are clearly not ready for a relationship, and the signs are ignored in the beginning. Years later, their marriage ends because of infidelity or simply because someone was not quite ready for the relationship. It is okay to take time, whether you are a man or a woman, to make sure you are ready to be exclusive with another person. More importantly, people change all of the time so you have to be willing to let people change and accept change. The worst thing I have done and have even seen other women do is wait for a man while he does whatever he wants to do. We sit around thinking that he is going to change his cheating, his lazy ways, his lying, or his entire self. I have always been told if it is meant to be then it will be, but when we interfere and try to force something to happen it will eventually be destroyed anyway.

Consider the woman who has a man who sits at home all of the time. Day after day he says he is going to find a job and help take care of the family, but weeks, months, and even years have passed and he has yet to find a job and work like a real man because he has neglected to be responsible and instead chooses to be lazy. This is a situation where a young man is not taking the necessary steps to fulfill his obligations as a man and prefers to remain in the period as a boy. The woman, however, encourages his behavior because she refuses to stand firm and reject his laziness. She is tricked into believing he will she will train him to become a man. Obviously, her methods are not working because she is trying to turn a boy into a man. You cannot feed a growing child baby food forever because eventually you have to feed him adult food to provide nourishment and nutrients to help the child grow. The same is true with men and women. If you are constantly feeding your mates baby food that will only stunt his growth, then do not expect him to act like a man. Sometimes we can influence boys to grow up and be a man, but all in all they have to take the necessary steps to become a man.

Think about your situation. Are you truly happy with him hitting on you? Do you really feel empowered as the strong and courageous woman you were created to be? How many times will you make excuses for him cheating? How many times will you give him chance after chance to get it together? How many times will you allow him to convince you he is grown and mature? So many women feel it is good enough to be with a young boy, instead of waiting for the man God wants to bless us with. Please know that a boy's love is nothing like a man's love.

Boys vs. Men

When you experience the love of a real man, you can clearly see the differences between a boy's love and a man's love. A boy will only be concerned with himself, while a man will sacrifice himself to show how much he loves you. A boy will expect you to always take care of you, while a man's love will cause you to want to take care of him because he in turn takes care of you. A boy will whine and cry and argue over the petty things, while a man will communicate effectively, share his feelings, and listen to you when you speak. A boy will call you to make sure you are where you say you are or to keep tabs on you, while a man will show his love by calling just to say he loves you or is thinking about you. A boy will be quick to chase after any female that gives him any kind of attention, but a man will not have time for another woman because all of his attention will be focused on you. A boy will treat you any kind of way, disrespect you, and react without thinking like a toddler on a playground, while a man's love will never allow him to say or do anything disrespectful because like a rare diamond he refuses to destroy or harm something so priceless. As you choose your next mate or analyze your current relationship, consider the differences between a boy's love and a man's love. Determine if the love is childish and boyish-like, or if it is the precious, strong, caring, compassionate, and sensual love of a real man.

Reality Speaks: Puppy love is for children, but a mature woman needs love from a mature man.

Realistic Thinking

**Can you tell the difference between a man's love and boy's love?
List some differences.**

Man's Love	Boy's Love

Reality Checkpoint #10—Over thirty (30) and worried.

Consider your age right now, whether you are younger than thirty or over the age of thirty. When you were a child what did you think you would be doing or have by now? What were your hopes and dreams? For some, your dreams have become a reality and you feel you are right on track as related to your plans for your life. For others, your dreams have yet to come true and you are on the brinks of losing hope for any type of future. You have yet to find your dream career, your business has not started, you did not receive the loan for the house, your name is not known nationally across the United States, and you have yet to find, of course, your dream husband. Some may not even think they are on track to finding their dream husband because they have yet to find a boyfriend. When it comes to finding the dream husband at times this seems like the most difficult thing to come across throughout the course of our lives even though he's supposed to find us. We may have the house, the career, the friends, but we do not have the dream husband and family we have always dreamed about.

Dreams vs. Reality

As I think back to when I was a child, I remember, and most women also remember, dreaming about the "perfect" husband, getting married, starting a family, and living happily ever after. Of course the Cinderella, Prince Charming, and even the Little Mermaid movies inspired some of my dreams and aspirations. As I got older I was influenced by some of my favorite movies like Love Jones, The Best Man, and even Brown Sugar. As I watched the Best Man and Love Jones I was given hope of making a relationship last even through the thick and thin. When I watched Brown Sugar I realized that if love were meant to be then it would be and how true love will find itself. All of these things and other influencers inspired me to have the same things. Even because of the absence of my earthly father I was convinced that my children would not grow up without a caring and loving father, so I understood the importance of wanting a good man in my life. Nonetheless, I soon realized that all of the movies I watched, although based on real life experiences, were just that—movies. Real life is much different from the movies. Sometimes we get caught up in our own plans and forget that it is not the movies that control every part of our destiny. Our plans may be different from what God has for us, and until we walk in His plans for our lives we will waste seconds, minutes, and even a lifetime.

As women, it was natural for us to say we would be married by the age of 25 and have kids by the age of 30. We had it all worked out. We would graduate from high school, attend College/trade School or start working, complete our post-secondary plans, and finally marry our Mr. Right. As time passed, we soon realized plans were not going as expected. It seemed like it was rare to find humble, honorable, honest, and hard-working men. Time was passing by and the dream of having a good husband was slowly disappearing because to have a husband meant you first had to have a boyfriend, and that seemed impossible. For some women this is their mentality even now. Over 30 and worried refers to those women, whether younger or older than 30, who have endured a number of relationships and have yet to find Mr. Right. These women are worried because they think their Mr. Right is in outer space or nowhere to be found. They have lost hope on starting their wonderful family because of the hurt, pain, and frustration they have experienced for some time now.

Why are we over (or under) 30 and worried?

What causes us to be over 30 and worried? What causes us to think we have to be married by a certain age in order to experience happiness and fulfillment? One of the reasons why we become over 30 and worried is mainly because of our bad experiences with relationships. We have dated and dated until we cannot date anymore. We have dated the good guys, the bad guys, the down low guys, the cheating guys, the lying guys, the "want to play games all of the time" guys, the "I'm not ready for marriage" guys, the too conceited guys, the abusive guys, the guys who are afraid to love, and the guys who just wanted to be every woman's man guy. After experiencing all of the different relationships some have determined that love just does not live in their homes. There was a time when I lost hope after dating a plethora of men because I was fed up. Until I met my soul mate, every man I dated had lied, cheated, were not on my level or vice versa, or disrespected me in some way. Although I experienced a lot of pain and suffering, it was not fair for me to blame every guy for all of the problems because I was not always smart when it came time to choose the type of guys I dated.

Another reason we become over 30 and worried is because of our friends and others around us. We see the couples in the mall or the grocery store and start thinking about when the time will happen for us. We attend multiple weddings in a year, and even play the role as a bridesmaid in our friends' weddings. Some of our friends may even be younger, so even then we feel especially hopeless. "Even my younger sister or girlfriend is getting married before me," is what we tell ourselves. We think because everyone else is on the road toward marriage then it is time we should be on the same track. What we fail to understand, however, is the fact that everyone has a different life path. What may be right for her at that moment may not be right for you right now. We compare our lives to everyone else's and get worried because we think we will never experience the same happiness and love.

Another reason we become over 30 and worried is simply because we position our minds and focus on nothing else except for finding the right man. We become so obsessed with trying to find a man that it becomes the main focus in our lives. We live, eat, breathe, and sleep men. When we talk, all we talk about is men. When we dream all we dream about are men. We act in a way that will only bring attention from a man whether positive or negative attention.

Sometimes the focus is merely based on having the dream wedding and not the marriage in order to create the illusion of being happily in love for others to see. I have seen so many women make the wedding the focal point of their lives and neglect the important components that make up a relationship. They soon forget that the wedding cannot or should not take place when two people are not truly in love. Love is what brings two people together, but some ignore the feeling of love or disguise it with lust and money just to make sure the wedding takes place. Years later in the marriage you realize that the wedding should not have taken place anyway because love was never a part of the relationship. The wedding lasts for a moment, but the marriage lasts for a lifetime. The wedding allows you to display an act of love toward the person even if you do not love them, but a marriage requires you to love the person no matter what. The wedding is a celebration where people can have fun, but the marriage may require stability during the times when it seems like there is nothing to celebrate. The wedding brings all types of people around who care about you and want to share in the celebration, but the marriage may bring about people who want to destroy your relationship instead of help it. Basically ladies, we have to remember that the marriage requires work, patience, and love, and we cannot think having merely a wedding will automatically cause a life-time of happiness. Make sure your dreams do not only revolve around the wedding day because if you think your marriage only begins on the day of the wedding, then you can count on the marriage ending on the same day of the wedding.

Naturally, we even become over 30 and worried because we acknowl-edge that our biological clock for reproducing children is running out of time. We used to dream about the big house, with a white picket fence, and our children running around in the yard. We pictured our children playing peewee football or participating in cheerleading, but now the dream seems out of reach. Children were always thought to be a part of our future, but now as we approach our late twenties, 30's, 40's, or even 50's we think it will be impossible to reproduce children. Of course it is natural to be concerned with having children at an older age because of the major health risks, but it still should not cause us to rush into any and every type of relationship. We have to know that although the plan has not come to fruition it just may be on delay. What we think is impos-sible, God can make possible. Even if you are older and concerned with children, God can make a way for you to have a wonderful husband and a family.

Consequences of your worrying

What exactly happens when we are over 30 and worried? Some decide to give up on love completely and decide they will never ever experi-ence a real relationship. Others decide to make it happen no matter what they have to do even if it means staying in a relationship that is not healthy or adds no value to their lives. Let us take a look at the woman who decides to give up. She becomes like the lonely woman who speaks loneliness into her life because she is hopeless about the situation of finding a good man. She has experienced a variety of relationships with a variety of different men. Those past men are often referred to as dogs, and she considers them worthless because they did not satisfy her wants and needs as she imagined. In the end, they all turned out to be nothing. The first one lied and said he was single, but later found out he was married the entire time. The second one was okay, but he was always involved with baby mama drama and she could not deal with all of that. The next one seemed nice in the beginning, but in the end he turned out to be mean and nasty. The next one was a habitual liar and could never be trusted about anything. Another guy was cute and charming, but loved to charm even her friends behind her back. The one after him just seemed crazy because he would call of the time. He was controlling, and just too needy. Another one used her for her body, and had no interest in getting to know her mind, body, and soul. One of the last guys was cute but he was so boring, and they had nothing in common. They could not force compatibility if they wanted to because they were just too different. Even in the midst of breakups and fallouts, guys that she tried to date were not what she wanted. None of them fit the prototype of her soul mate.

Nonetheless, as she exits each relationship and enters a new one she gains the attitude that a woman over 30 and worried (or younger) would naturally have. She gains bitterness in her heart for those men who lied and cheated and said they only wanted to be with her. The bitterness eventually turns to rage or vengeance and she decides to hurt people in the same way. She thinks every man is locked up and behind bars in a prison so she feels the need to turn to a woman because the choices for a good man are slim to none. She thinks there is no man out there on her level because she went to college and has a successful career, so she hides herself behind her work in an attempt to ignore her desire to be with a man. She realizes how much men have used her and decides to use men in the same way to get money, clothes, and anything she wants. Not only is this type of woman affecting her lifestyle and attitude, but she is also affecting others. She becomes so set in her ways and refuses to accept that any man will ever be a good man. She constantly states, "There are no good men. All men are dogs. Men only want one thing. All men are worthless, or I do not need a man in my life." It is true that you do not need a man to give you things you can give yourself like happiness, self-love, confidence, courage, beauty, and even success. However, for many there will come a time when you will want a wonderful marriage and not just a wedding. You will want a beautiful family and not just a baby daddy. You will want a romantic getaway without the guilt of participating in sexual sin all of the time, and for all of these things you will need a man to complete these tasks. If you are content with being single for the rest of your life, then be content and happy with your status. Nevertheless, if you know deep down inside that God has a husband waiting for you then eliminate the pessimistic attitude of feeling like you will never find a good man. There is power in your tongue and you have to speak life to your dead situations. Yes, you may have been in bad relationships and you feel frustrated because it seems like Mr. Right is non-existent, but you have to trust that God will send Mr. Right when the time is right. God is not always saying no, He may just be saying not yet.

Think about it. If he sent you Mr. Right today, would you be ready and willing to accept Him? Or would you be so bitter, heartbroken, and stuck in the past that you would not know what to do with Mr. Right? You could drive him away with all of your negativity and focus on those things that happened in your past. Mr. Right could come along right in front of your face and you would not know what to do because your mind already thinks Mr. Right does not exist. If you think he does not exist, then he will not exist because your eyes, mind, and heart will be closed to anything and anyone that even appears to love you for you and for no other reason. You have to make sure your self-love is present before God can send you a mate who will love you. If you lack self-love, then you will not allow anyone else to love because you will think no one else is capable of loving you. You will feel as if you do not deserve love.

It is easy to have bitterness and anger toward the men of our pasts, but have you ever considered why you chose the men you dated in your past? Were you with him for his style or his sensitivity? Did you enjoy his passionate kisses, or were you intrigued by his passion for you? Were you just interested in his looks, or did you look more on the inside to really figure out what type of man he was? As women, we tend to think with only our feelings and we ignore what our minds may be telling us. We think to ourselves, "I know he cheats and lies from time to time, but he is so sweet and does anything for me, and he is so cute. He understands me." Well, if he really understands you then he would understand that you do not enjoy being lied to. He should understand your worth and your dignity. It is easy to blame them for all of our ruined relationships, but remember it was you who ultimately decided to be with the different guys.

Furthermore, sometimes we date men who are just there for a reason or a season. Usually we learn from them the type of man we truly desire. We learn the personality, the character, and the values we desire from a real man. Obviously, it was not meant for you to be with those past men because somewhere along the line there were too many differences that prohibited a successful relationship. Even all of the hurt and pain should not cause you to completely give up because even hurt and pain has its purpose. Nonetheless, some of the hurt and pain you endured could have occurred merely because of your mistakes and your willingness to be with any and everyone. Now, you become over 30 and worried when you should have been under 30 and unworried. You endured pain you should have let go of a long time ago, or you allowed different situations to take place repeatedly. You have to take responsibility for those things you allowed to occur. Ladies, you cannot dwell on your past sufferings for a lifetime and expect to overcome being over 30 and worried.

Keep Pushing!

Bishop T.D. Jakes likes to refer to the pain and suffering we experience in different types of relationships to an analogy describing the pain and suffering a mother experiences during child birth. He encouraged me so much through one of his books when I was experiencing some heartache. He referred to the agony as the severe pain a mother experiences during the birth. For moments and even long hours, a mother endures strenuous pain and soreness to push the baby through the birth canal. As soon as the baby comes forth, all of the pain and suffering is forgotten and replaced with tears of joy because of the beautiful person she now cares for and loves. She cherishes this new life and promises to take care of this God-given life. He told me, in his own words, to keep pushing because I was about to give birth to something new that would bring joy and happiness. So, I tell you in the same way to KEEP PUSHING! PUSH until your husband comes and wait patiently for the arrival. PUSH until you are satisfied with your new career or business. PUSH your way through the obstacles and pray to God to help you through it all to make sure He receives the glory and honor, and everything goes according to His will. Some like to refer to PUSH as pray until something happens, but not only do you need to pray until something happens but you also have to work until something happens. You have to work to make sure you grow and develop a better you in all areas of your life. When searching for a job, it is not enough to just pray and hope that a job will come out of nowhere. Instead, you have to do the preliminary work—resumes, networking, interviewing, etc.—to prepare for your next move.

Anything good in life is worth the struggle because in the end you will be more appreciative because of the hard work you put into it. Whether it is a new career, a new car, your new business, or your new man, you may have to endure some pain and suffering along the way, but this pain will only last for a season. When your true love comes into your life and shows the true meaning of love you will soon forget all of the hurt and pain you endured because you will feel so overwhelmed with love, grace, and happiness. If you are enduring pain even right now as you read this book thinking about your ex's and how he does not love you anymore, know that your pain will only last for a moment. You can get out of the depressive and sorrowful state and claim victory over your situation.

Understand, however, that although newborns and new men can bring you joy, they are not the ultimate source of your joy for God is the source of our joy. You have to cast your cares upon Him and rely on Him to take the hurt and pain away, and He will give you a new joy that only He can provide. He will give you hope and reassure you that you will be blessed with a good husband. His joy will allow you to smile and feel renewed even when you walk through the mall and see your ex with his new girlfriend. His joy will make you smile even when you see him for the first time in weeks, months, or years and you are still cordial and polite to him. His joy will remind you that God cherishes every single thing about you even when your ex continuously ignores you and treats you as if you never meant anything to him. His joy will allow you to feel good when you are home alone with no one to hold, so you can enjoy a good movie or television show all by yourself. His joy will allow you to feel secure with whatever your current situation may be and no matter what others may think of your situation.

Worrying is useless

You can be over 30 and NOT WORRY. Other words/phrases used to describe worry include: anxiety, fret, troubled, lack of sleep, fear, nervousness, or apprehension. If you experience all of these emotions solely due to the lack of having a man, then your priorities are all out of order. Your nervousness and fear stems from the thought of never experiencing real love and being alone for the rest of your life. You constantly have feelings of anxiety and may even lose sleep because you think you will never find a man. Note, however, that you are the cause for the worry and distraught because you do not trust the Lord to do a new work in you. In Matthew, it teaches us that God even cares about the flowers and the birds, so of course he cares about His children. Worrying does not add another minute, another day, and it will not add another man to your life. Your ex's and past relationships are right where they belong, in the past. So, why are you still living in the past and not concentrating optimistically on the future? Worrying is obviously not healthy because as mentioned before it can cause some to lose sleep and have severe anxiety. If you are included in this category, stay over 30 but please lose the worry. You are too beautiful, too intelligent, and too wonderful of a person to spend so much of your time worrying about who your next mate will be. Spend your time planning your next move in life. Construct a program to help people in need, and/or to find more time to minister to those who are lost. "An idle mind is the devil's playground." If a parent takes a glimpse off of their son/daughter while they are on the playground, the child is at risk of finding other playmates that will influence bad behavior. The children will even forget about their parents and get too caught up in having fun. Just like that young child, you too can get caught up with bad influencers and lose sight of the one who really cares about you. Nonetheless, you do not want the devil to play around in your life causing you to play yourself. It will appear to be a game between you and the devil, but eventually the fun will end and you will need to find the real source of your joy.

You are probably thinking even right now, "S. Marie, you do not even know what I have been through. Even my friends have not been successful when it comes to men. Good men just do not exist anymore. I have looked everywhere and have yet to find a good man". Well, guess what. I used to think the same things and I have been through the same things. I have been through situations, and I felt all types of feelings from hurt, pain, to frustration and bitterness. I was convinced that all men were dogs and they were never going to be a part of my life. I gave up trying to look for a man and decided I would just be by myself. Ironically, my heart was in the wrong place but my actions were not. Alone time is exactly what I needed in order to know what God wanted for me and so I would have the chance to get to know myself before trying to be with someone else. To be honest, in the back of my mind I knew God had something in store for me and I was finally willing to wait for Him to do His work without my interruptions. I was still hesitant, naturally, but ultimately I turned my hopelessness into hopefulness because I knew God had control over my destiny. What I thought was hopeless and over, eventually turned into something much more.

It took a lot of faith and submission to do His will for me to reach that point. I had been with the liars, cheaters, adulterers, and others but I knew I could not let my past ruin my future. My mindset changed and I made sure I remained positive about the future no matter what the outcome was going to be. I could no longer act as if men were the enemy; rather I had to acknowledge that men are humans just as I am, and we all make mistakes. I refused to have the mindset of a woman over 30 and worried because I knew I believed I would be over thirty and happy.

I met my soul mate as soon as I let go of feelings of despair, sadness, and bitterness. I stopped thinking all hope was lost, and instead I focused more on spending time with Christ and developing myself to become more of a virtuous woman. By this time I knew exactly what I wanted and my soul mate was everything and more. Of course the beginning had its ups and downs as we were trying to get to know each other, but it was nothing like my past relationships. That, of course, happens when two people are trying to get to know each other. Nevertheless, I felt something like I had never felt before. I used to hear all of the time how when you meet your soul mate you just know. I can say with all sincerity and love that I know my soul mate is a Godsend. He is everything and more than I could ever imagine. I've cried, people have betrayed me, I've been lied to, and I've been hurt more than one time. Nonetheless, I am thankful and praising God because I kept pushing, and now the end result is here—my husband. Moreover, I did not pursue him; rather he pursued me and he definitely proved to me that he was a good man. He knew in the beginning what I expected out of him (and vice versa), and we were both willing to meet those expectations. If he says he will do something, he will do it. He doesn't simply talk the talk, but his actions reflect his words. There is nothing like the warmth and secure feeling of being in love with a man who in turn reciprocates the love back to you. The journey seemed long at times, but all in all everything I went through just prepared me even more for what was to come. It was the end to the pain that led to the beginning of a new life with the one and only true love of my life.

Desperately in love

The other over 30 and worried woman decides to take her energy and work tirelessly to make sure she finds Mr. Right. She is willing to do whatever it takes to make sure she will find Mr. Right before she gets too old. Unlike the bitter and vengeful woman, she has no plans of getting even, and she is totally convinced that she will get married no matter what. She knows Mr. Right exists even if he is not Mr. Right. The first problem, however, is the fact that she is looking for Mr. Right instead of having Mr. Right look for her. I have seen desperation in so many forms. She either takes it to the club every day of the week or every weekend, or she stays with some guy whom she knows is totally not for her. Being over 30 and worried causes us to act out of feelings instead of using our minds. We become involved in situations that cause us to take desperate measures. We think we have to commit all of our time and effort in order to avoid being over 30 and worried. However, even if you are younger than 30 and most of your attention is focused on finding your husband then you are already over 30 and worried because you have taken matters into your own hands. Release the hold you have on the situation so God can take control over your life. Remove yourself from the situation if you know he is not the one. Quit going to the wrong places every 5 seconds thinking you will one day find your Mr. Right. Quit taking desperate measures by forcing something out of nothing. Quit thinking just because you have a baby with him he will want to be with you for the rest of your life. Quit pressuring him to be with you and marry you when you know inside you just want to have a pretty wedding so you will be the first to get to married. Quit being so desperate and start being determined and dedicated to living the life God has planned for you.

Own up to it!

Ladies, the message is so clear—we have to take ownership of our own mistakes and acknowledge that we cannot blame our male partners for everything that takes place in our lives. You have to pick up the broken pieces and move on and declare that you will be blessed whether you are with a man or not. Quit blaming him for all of your problems and acknowledge that you have not always been the best woman you could have been. Yes, he may have caused you hurt and pain but it is you who decides the outcome of the situation. You can sob and cry forever, or you can move on toward something greater. Men and women will cause hurt and pain in our lives, but we have to help each other and not judge their actions all of the time because we are all humans. You may be the liar, the cheater, or the evil one in the relationship so maybe you need to do a self-evaluation.

Sometimes, the relationship ended because you needed to be alone, you needed to get your priorities in order, or the timing just was not right. If God tells you to release and to get rid of things that are hindering your growth but you ignore Him, then He may do what He has to do to get rid of it even when you resist. How many times did you stay with someone and you knew God was telling you to leave? Resisting His guidance will restrict your growth. Thank Him for removing that guy who you knew was taking advantage of you. Thank Him for removing the man who was one more incident away from giving you an STD. Thank Him for removing the man who continuously abused you. Thank Him for removing the man who repeatedly fooled you and betrayed your trust through lies and deceit. Thank Him for removing those things in your life that you did not have the strength yourself to say no to. God knew you needed to let it go and He knew you would gain even more than what you lost. God loves us so much that even He can see when we are digging ourselves into the deepest hole, but He still finds a way to bring us out of it even when we refuse the help. Only love would do something so great.

Women, we can no longer go around thinking and saying that all men are bad and that all they want to do is hurt women. All men are not dogs. Blaming other people for everything that happens in our lives is the easy way out because then we can ignore our mistakes and shortcomings by focusing on others. That is why people gossip so much. They are either jealous or they just feel the need to focus their attention on someone else so they can feel better about themselves. If you do not take time and really consider the things you did wrong in your broken relationships then you will not be able to improve yourself. Our thoughts and minds have to change, which will influence our actions, and change our reactions. For example, if you think you will be blessed to find a husband and you know it is in God's will, then your actions will not reflect actions of a desperate woman in need of a man. Your actions will reflect a woman on a mission to do God's will, instead of reflecting a woman sitting around waiting on a man to come and do what only she can do for herself. When a man tells you he does not want to be with you anymore or he would rather just be a friend, you will react with a calm and dignified spirit instead of overreacting. You will no longer think you are losing everything through your acknowledgement of having everything through Christ. If you know you have a pessimistic and unenthusiastic attitude, then you need to ask for a renewing of your mind. Change the way you think and you will see a change in your life. It is just like a successful business owner. There was a day or a moment when he/she thought of the idea for starting a new business and eventually his thoughts came to fruition. The business never would have come into existence if the thought process had not taken place first. The actor would have never won the Oscar if they had not envisioned accomplishing more. The teacher never would have entered the classroom if he/she hadn't proclaimed that they would influence and impact the lives of young people. You will never receive the fullness of life until you begin to think, speak, and act as if your life is already fulfilled.

For so long, ladies, I blamed everyone else for all of my relationships and decided that it was everyone else who caused my hurt and pain. For so long I was unhappy because I could not find a man, or I could not keep a man. I felt like I was being too nice and easygoing, when in actuality I was just too naïve and easygoing with the wrong men. I was confused as to why I kept attracting Mr. Wrong, or why Mr. Wrong kept finding a way to charm me. Finally, reality checked in and I realized I was guilty of every reality checkpoint at some time or another in my life. It all makes sense because now I fully understood that not everything I experienced could be attributed to a man. I did not beat myself up with feelings and guilt and shame; rather, after carefully analyzing myself and my actions I decided to change my thinking, my actions and interactions with men, and my entire lifestyle.

---

*Reality Speaks: I don't know anything, but, Lord, you know everything.
So, why worry?*

__Realistic Thinking__

How do you usually react when you are worried about something?

_____
_____
_____
_____
_____
_____
_____
_____

How has worrying, about anything, affected your thoughts, heart, or even your life?

_____
_____
_____
_____
_____
_____
_____
_____

Instead of worrying, I would rather ....

_____
_____
_____
_____
_____
_____
_____
_____
_____
_____
_____
_____
_____
_____

Reality Check 101

Women, whether lonely or loving, single or married, young or grown and sexy, we have to take control over our lives with God in the captain's seat. We must prevent other people and situations from guiding how we live. Do a reality check and figure out if you are preventing Mr. Right from coming into your life. You are still single, but really think about why you are still single. Use all of the reality checkpoints and really be honest with yourself. One of the most difficult things for a human to do is admit when they are or have done wrong, but once you keep it real with yourself, then you will be able to keep it real with everyone else around you.

First of all, make sure you are doing God's thing instead of making your man everything. He knows the plan for your life so if you are not on track with what He has in store for you, then the rest of your life's plans will be completely rerouted. It is so easy for us to do what we think is best, but be sure you consult with God first to make sure that is actually the best. You may think it is a good idea to be a with a man so you can get married and have a family, but it is not a good idea to be with a man who is already married and has a family. Your plan is not in the will of God, and does not coincide with the caring and loving person you are. For example, if you are the woman right now holding onto someone else's man, let him go and release him back to his family. You cannot afford for your husband to do the same thing to you and potentially destroy your future relationship. Consider his wife and his kids' feelings before you decide to take something that rightfully belongs to someone else. If you have God as your captain and follow His instructions, then you will avoid the path towards destruction. Even if you happen to lose your way along the journey, ask for His help and strength so you can get back on the right track. Do not take the chance of giving up on your future by giving up on the one who holds the key to your destiny.

Secondly, remember what true love is and do not confuse it with sex. Refer to the passage below taken from 1 Corinthians chapter 13 (NKJV):

4 Love suffers long and is kind; love does not envy; love does not parade itself, is not puffed up; 5 does not behave rudely, does not seek its own, is not provoked, thinks no evil; 6 does not rejoice in iniquity, but rejoices in the truth; 7 bears all things, believes all things, hopes all things, endures all things.
8 Love never fails …

First Corinthians is one of the best passages that explain the true meaning of love. This passage speaks of being kind and lacks envy. If you have a man and you are jealous all of the time, you are confusing your feelings with love. If you think evil thoughts or seek your own agenda, then you are confused about love. It mentions how love does not rejoice in iniquity (sin) but instead rejoices in the truth. Lies and deceit are not worth rejoicing in any type of relationship. Toward the end of the excerpt it explains that love endures all things. Ask yourself, will your love endure and prevail when the sex is gone? If your answer is no, then you are confusing love with sex. Never once does it refer to love as sex, or mention that having a lot of sex means you are really in love. Sex does not mean you are in love and you have to make sure you do not confuse the two, because if you do then you could end up with someone who will seem to care more about you when you are in the bed than when you are not in the bed. Sex is to be shared between a man and his wife and the act of sex should not be taken lightly. Young ladies, little Timmy is not interested in being committed so do not think that your having sex with him will make them love you any more than you think they do. Women, quit thinking he will only be with you if you engage in sexual relations. You know ultimately that is not what you want. If you are truly serious about making a lifestyle change, then you will make the change. A new level of growth will cause a new level of intimacy in your relationship. Try it and you will see. More importantly, don't do it just because I say so, but do it because God knows what is best for you. He wants you to live your life to the fullest, and prevent it from having moments of pleasure that will cause a lifetime of consequences.

Thirdly, ladies, quit blaming your present mate for mistakes that occurred in your past. Your present man could be the one for you, but you may be overshadowing his efforts with the actions of your previous guys. As Musiq Soulchild said, "I'm not to blame for the pain that was caused by previous cats that had your heart before me." He was so honest and correct when he wrote those lyrics because that is exactly what we do. We try to transfer our anger and bitterness toward our new man when he had nothing to do with the hurt and pain in the first place. If you keep clogging up your heart with ill-will feelings, you will soon suffer from congestive heart failure, which will prevent you from ever loving again. Be aware of your feelings and make sure you truly let go before you try to move on. He has to know you want to move forward, and that you are no longer interested in staying behind.

Fourthly and fifthly, quit thinking you can mold him into the type of person you want him to be and stop trying to change a man into a boy. If you know you are not in the right type of relationship then remove yourself from the situation. Do not go on any longer wasting time by thinking he will change when he is not ready to change. When he is ready to change he will change. You cannot force someone to do something when they are not willing and ready to do it. Accept the things you cannot change, and gain the courage to change the things you can change.

Next, you must remember not to try and keep up with the Joneses—also known as your girlfriends/friends—all of the time. What God has for you is specifically for you, and what He has for your friends is what He has for your friends. Do not get caught up in trying to keep up with their lifestyles but encourage each other and celebrate each other's accomplishments. If you can celebrate in their joy and happy moments, then you can stand to be blessed in the same way.

Ladies, remember to create standards and realistic expectations. Avoid excessive ultimatums that only provide benefits for one of the partners. Stand strong by your standards and refuse to settle. When you settle you limit the potential to a full and prosperous life because you lower your standards and accept anything that comes your way. Even as you stand firm on your standards, you still need to open yourself to compromise and agreements. There will be things about each other you will like, and there will be things about each other you do not like. All in all, you have to be open and willing to talk about the areas that need improvement. For example, if he says all you do is nag and tell him how he never does anything right, then maybe you are guilty of that. No man wants to feel like he isn't doing anything for his woman, so sometimes you might have to encourage him more and learn how to communicate more effectively. If you know you enjoy spending time with your family and friends, you should understand that he wants to spend time his family and friends also. Overall, do not ask him to do something you would not be willing to do. Communicate with each other to ensure both parties have a clear understanding of what is expected in the relationship to eliminate unexpected surprises.

To my over-thirty and worried ladies and "I think therefore I am—lonely" women, change your mindset by replacing the negative notions with positive perceptions. You have to see your husband and your family in your life by having faith despite your circumstances. The more you think you are lonely, the more you will feel as if you are truly alone when in actuality you are not alone. The more you worry about finding a real man, the less time you will spend developing the real woman inside of you. Know that loneliness and worry are not good for one's health because they each can lead to a depressive and dismal state of mind. Use the time, however, to grow as a woman by spending time with yourself and God. You would be surprised to know how much you learn about yourself while spending alone time. You learn your strengths and your weaknesses and find ways to improve yourself. Then, when Mr. Right comes along you will be ready and prepared to be a good woman to a good man. Only God can make the impossible possible, and he can bless you when you and the timing are right simultaneously.

Lastly, ladies, we have to make sure we are looking and waiting for the right thing. If you continuously chase after the money, the mansions, the clothes, the shoes, and mo' money, then that is exactly what you will end up with. In your possession you will have all of the material things you crave, but you will never possess the love of a real man. You will be in a relationship where he spends about 1% of his time with you during the week, but spends 100% of his money on you and your shopping sprees every week. He will pay your bills but will refuse to pay you any attention. For some women, they are totally fine with this lifestyle. For the ones who are faking this lifestyle and acting like they are okay with being a gold digger or being pimped, stop faking your way through life and become the real and virtuous woman you were created to be as described in the book of Proverbs (NKJV).

Although the virtuous woman may appear to have qualities you may lack, she is the woman every woman should aspire to be. None of us are perfect, and we cannot think we are ever too old to stop growing. When we think we have reached our growth potential, we limit our potential to become better than good—great. There is no greater example of a woman who truly represents the essence of womanhood. As you come into the new beginnings of your life, and I believe in my heart you want a new beginning, remember the qualities and character of a virtuous woman. If you cannot be the virtuous woman God designed you to be, then how can you possibly become a virtuous wife? As you wait for your husband to come along, remember to use your time wisely and develop yourself into a virtuous woman so you will be the virtuous wife he will need. Based on the passage, you will show him you are trustworthy by being loyal and faithful. Your actions will only bring good in his life, not harm, even when he makes you upset. You will refuse the spirit of idleness to make sure your husband and family are taken care of. Your words will bring wisdom and kindness instead of bitterness and anger. Everything about you will be righteous and upright, which will be passed along to your children. Be careful, however, along the journey because a virtuous woman does not qualify every man as an honorable and honest man. There will be those who will come along disguised as your true love, but trust and know your true love will find you and you will recognize him.

As you continue your journey towards love, remember to take ownership of your mishaps and errors, and start today by trying to correct them. All of us have made mistakes, and all of us need to work hard to improve our inner beauty. Realize, realign, and reposition yourself. Once you realize you cannot change what happened in the past, you will be able to realign your goals and focus. Then, you will be able to reposition yourself in a way that aligns with God's will. Now is the time, if you haven't done so already, to begin your self-evaluation in order to make changes where necessary, so, when Mr. Right comes along you will be ready. As painful or challenging it may have been, you've thought about every relationship or experience you've been through, but now is the time to look forward. Your past and present situation cannot determine your future destination. Observe what occurred and take notice so things will be different. The realization may cause the transformation for your situation.

Wake up, girlfriend and keep it real! You've been sleeping for too long. Just like you experience different storms in your life for different reasons, there are different reasons for everyone's singleness. He left you or you left him. God removed him from your life, or you removed him on your own will. The timing isn't right and you actually prefer to be single. Maybe you're just tired of dealing with dead end relationships, and you've just given up all hope. Nevertheless, your current situation can in fact change. You don't have to remain single forever if you change the things you have the control to change. No matter when and no matter what happened, there's a reason why you're single, but YOU don't have to be the reason.

Reality Speaks: The realization may cause the transformation for your situation. There's a reason why you're single, but you don't have to be the reason.

Realistic Thinking: I may have contributed to the reasons why I'm single, but what am I going to do about it now? Based on my willingness to confront real issues I didn't want to admit, how do I feel? More importantly, what will I improve and be mindful of the next time before entering into a relationship?

_____

_____

_____

_____

_____

_____

_____

_____

_____

_____

_____

_____

_____

_____

_____

_____

_____

_____

_____

_____

_____

_____

_____

_____

_____

_____

_____

_____

_____

978-0-595-48480-5
0-595-48480-8